New Seaside Interiors
Nouveaux intérieurs de la côte

New Seaside Interiors

Nouveaux intérieurs de la côte

Edited by | Sous la direction de | Herausgegeben von
Angelika Taschen

Text by | Texte de | Text von
Ian Phillips

TASCHEN

HONG KONG KÖLN LONDON LOS ANGELES MADRID PARIS TOKYO

Endpapers | Pages de garde | Vorsatz:
Gianna & Theodore Angelopoulos, Mykonos, Greece
Photo: Marina Faust
Pages 2/3: A house with a view, Eyjafjordur, Iceland
Photo: Gunnar Sverrisson
Pages 4/5: Lifeguard tower by architect Ulrich Müther, Binz/Rügen, Germany
Photo: Christian Kerber
Pages 6/7: Paul Barthelemy, Alicudi, Italy
Photo: Giorgio Possenti/Vega MG
Pages 8/9: Infinity Pool, Costa Brava, Spain
Photo: Jean-Luc Laloux
Pages 10/11: Terrace of a Romantic Retreat, North Morocco
Photo: Vincent Knapp
Pages 12/13: Shore Chic, Martha's Vineyard, Massachusetts
Photo: Don Freeman
Pages 14/15: Ken Crosson, Coromandel Peninsula, New Zealand
Photo: Nathalie Krag/Production: Tami Christiansen
Page 16: Ocean view, Warrnambool, Australia
Photo: Jean-Luc Laloux
Page 21: Gianna & Theodore Angelopoulos, Mykonos, Greece
Photo: Marina Faust

© 2008 TASCHEN GmbH
Hohenzollernring 53, D-50672 Köln
www.taschen.com

© 2008 VG Bild-Kunst, Bonn for the works of Harry Bertoia, Edouard Cazaux,
Robert Indiana, Grete Jalk, Mathieu Matégot, Roberto-Sebastian Matta Echaurren,
Charlotte Perriand, Niki de Saint Phalle, Ludwig Mies van der Rohe,
Arne Haugen Sørensen, Frank Stella, Michael Wesely, Jinshi Zhu.
© 2008 Lucio Fontana by SIAE/ VG Bild-Kunst, Bonn for the work of Lucio Fontana.
© 2008 for the works of Charles and Ray Eames: Eames Office, Venice, CA,
www.eamesoffice.com
Compilation, editing & layout: Angelika Taschen, Berlin
General Project Manager: Stephanie Bischoff, Cologne
Text: Ian Phillips, Paris
French translation: Philippe Safavi, Paris
German translation: Ingrid Hacker-Klier, Hebertsfelden
Production: Thomas Grell, Cologne

Printed in China
ISBN 978-3-8365-0387-7
ISBN 978-3-8365-0477-5 (edition with French cover)

Contents
Sommaire
Inhalt

The magic of the sea
Preface by Angelika Taschen

La magie de la mer
Préface de Angelika Taschen

Die Magie des Meeres
Vorwort von Angelika Taschen

A house beside the sea! It is a dream that a great many people always have. Eight years ago, for the first time, I gave that dream visual form in a book, and since then people have often told me that simply looking at it was like a holiday by the seaside. It is a wonderful compliment, to be told that one has so inspired the imagination of others that for a while they forget their everyday lives and go on their travels, at least in their minds. I'm told that some have even been prompted by the book to buy a house by the sea and adopt ideas from our book for the interior.

Back in 2000 I was already concerned to show the widest possible range of living styles, in very different climate zones – from the humble fisherman's cottage to the luxury villa, from the Swedish island of Gotland to tropical Tahiti. The one thing all the houses had in common was that the sea played the lead part.

And in every one of the houses there were maritime motifs – quite apart from the magnificent view. Generally the colour scheme, almost always a dominant blue and white, was chosen to reflect the sea. The combination of colours may not seem particularly original, but it is always appropriate and it is most intriguing to see just how many variations are possible without it ever becoming dull. For me, the standard for unequalled virtuosity was set by architect Gio Ponti in the Hotel Parco dei Principi in Sorrento on the Gulf of Naples.

Other maritime elements include finds from the beach – ropes, driftwood, shells, stones and starfish. In our first book of Seaside Interiors I was especially struck, in a Uruguayan home, by a sofa made from a rowing-boat no longer watertight. The new owners had hung it from the ceiling with ropes, and filled it with mattresses and cushions. And so they had a place from which to watch the sunset, gently swinging. That sofa cost next to nothing, fitted the surroundings perfectly, looked good, and was both cosy and imaginative – a good example of the truth that a stylish, individual way of living does not presuppose a fat wallet.

Which houses, of the thousands and thousands of potential candidates, should one include in a book designed to have a sales life of over a decade in the global market? For one thing, the interiors

Une maison au bord de la mer ! Il y a huit ans de cela, j'ai présenté dans un livre ce dont rêvent tant de gens de par le monde. On m'a dit souvent depuis qu'il suffisait de contempler les photos pour avoir l'impression d'être en vacances. Quel compliment ! N'est-ce pas merveilleux de stimuler l'imagination des lecteurs de telle manière qu'ils oublient un moment leur train-train quotidien et voyagent dans leur tête ? Après avoir lu cet ouvrage, certains auraient même acheté une maison en bord de mer et l'auraient aménagée en s'inspirant d'idées qu'ils y auraient puisées.

En l'an 2000, j'avais déjà tenté de montrer le plus grand nombre possible d'habitations en tout genre et sous toutes les latitudes – de la cabane de pêcheur à la villa glamour, de l'île suédoise Gotland à la tropicale Tahiti. Le point commun de ces demeures est le fait que la mer y joue le rôle principal.

Ces maisons jouissent bien sûr d'une vue sublime sur la mer, mais la présence de celle-ci se manifeste aussi ailleurs. Ainsi la palette où dominent presque toujours le bleu et le blanc. Et même si cette combinaison de couleurs semble bien peu originale, elle est toujours adaptée et il est fascinant de constater combien de variations sont possibles sans que l'ensemble ne paraisse ennuyeux. Pour moi, l'architecte Gio Ponti reste inégalé en ce domaine avec ce qu'il a accompli dans l'Hotel Parco dei Principi à Sorrente, dans le golfe de Naples.

Et puis les trouvailles faites sur la plage enrichissent cette ambiance – les cordages, les bois échoués, les coquillages, les galets et les étoiles de mer. Je me souviens avoir été particulièrement impressionnée dans notre premier volume de « Seaside Interiors » par un canapé vu dans une maison en Uruguay. En fait il s'agissait d'une barque prenant l'eau que ses nouveaux propriétaires avaient suspendue avec des cordes au plafond et remplie de matelas et de coussins. Maintenant on peut regarder d'ici le coucher du soleil en se balançant doucement. Ce canapé n'a pratiquement rien coûté et est adapté à l'environnement ; en plus il est très beau, confortable et témoigne d'une belle inventivité. Ce qui prouve que point n'est besoin d'être riche pour vivre dans un décor personnalisé et qui a de la classe.

Ein Haus am Meer! Vor acht Jahren habe ich diesen ewigen Traum vieler Menschen erstmals in einem Buch visualisiert. Seither höre ich oft, dass allein schon das Betrachten des Bildbandes wie Ferien am Meer wirken würde. Es ist ein wunderbares Kompliment, die Fantasie von Lesern so zu beflügeln, dass sie eine Zeit lang ihren Alltagstrott vergessen und in ihrem Kopf auf Reisen gehen. Einige, so höre ich, soll das Buch sogar inspiriert haben, ein Haus am Meer zu kaufen und mit konkreten Ideen daraus einzurichten.

Schon im Jahr 2000 hatte ich versucht, möglichst viele Wohnvariationen in höchst unterschiedlichen Klimazonen zu zeigen – von der kleinen Fischerhütte bis zur glamourösen Villa, von der schwedischen Insel Gotland bis zum tropischen Tahiti. Was alle Häuser miteinander verbindet: Jedes Mal spielt das Meer die Hauptrolle.

Und in jedem der Häuser finden sich – außer einer großartigen Aussicht – weitere maritime Anklänge. Meist ist auch die Farbwahl auf das Meer bezogen, fast immer dominieren Blau und Weiß. Auch wenn diese Farbkombination wenig originell scheint: Sie passt immer, und es ist höchst faszinierend zu sehen, wie viele Variationen möglich sind, ohne dass es langweilig wird. Der Architekt Gio Ponti hat für mich dies bisher unübertroffen virtuos in dem Hotel Parco dei Principi in Sorrent am Golf von Neapel vorgemacht.

Weitere maritime Ingredienzien sind Fundstücke vom Strand – wie Taue, Treibhölzer, Muscheln, Steine und Seesterne. Besonders hat mir in unserem ersten Band „Seaside Interiors" ein Sofa in Uruguay imponiert, das ursprünglich mal ein leckes Ruderboot war. Die neuen Besitzer hatten es mit Tauen an der Decke befestigt und das Innere mit Matratzen und Kissen gefüllt. Sanft schaukelnd kann man nun von hier den Sonnenuntergang betrachten. Dieses Sofa hat fast nichts gekostet, passte in die Umgebung, sah sehr schön aus, war gemütlich und fantasievoll. Ein Beispiel dafür, dass Geld keineswegs eine Voraussetzung für stilvolles, individuelles Wohnen ist.

Welches von zigtausend möglichen Häusern soll man in ein Buch aufnehmen, das sich weltweit

should display creativity, delight in discovery, originality, and attention to detail. The owner of the house may be a wealthy art collector who can commission an interior designer heavily in demand all around the world, or a young family with no financial resources who use their imagination and do it themselves – that is immaterial. Ten years after a book or life-style magazine appears, it isn't hard to spot who's merely been following the trends and fashions promoted in countless publications instead of developing their own taste. Interiors quickly look dated. In choosing houses for our book, that is of course something we scrupulously avoid.

Another factor in the success of a book is variety. Yet another house with the "right" Damien Hirst on the wall and original Prouvé chairs around the table is simply a bore. A driftwood sculpture made by the children of the house, on the other hand, gives everything a lighter feel. So one basic rule is that it's the mix that makes the music.

For me, the choice and placing of the photos is always of paramount importance. Only if that is right will a book generate an atmosphere that can fuel emotions and inspire dreams. Though a sense of the whole must be palpable, no purpose is served by dutifully illustrating the entire house from top to bottom. A full-page photo of light hitting a glass of water can sometimes have a greater impact than meticulously showing the whole of a perfectly furnished living room. And then of course there is the question of your photographers and their interpretations. If you have a house photographed by three fine professionals, you feel as if you're looking at three completely different interiors – so a key decision is which photographer is best suited to which design style.

In recent years, dozens of interior styles have appeared and, just as quickly, disappeared. Nonetheless, the interiors of houses beside the sea are less affected by fashions than one might expect in the age of globalisation. In my view, this is because people long for the simple life. In the morning you catch the fish (or buy it in the port) that you intend to eat for lunch. You pass your time simply contemplating the sea. Many of these house owners refuse to have

Parmi les milliers d'habitations possibles, laquelle sélectionner pour la présenter dans un livre qui doit s'imposer plus d'une décennie sur le marché international ? D'abord elle devrait refléter l'esprit créatif, la curiosité, l'originalité et l'amour du détail de son propriétaire, qu'il s'agisse d'un collectionneur d'art très riche ayant commandé la décoration à un architecte d'intérieur travaillant dans le monde entier, ou d'une jeune famille sans grands moyens, qui construit tout elle-même avec beaucoup de fantaisie.

Dix ans après la parution du livre ou d'un magazine de décoration d'intérieur, on a vite fait de remarquer celui qui n'a fait que suivre l'un des trends propagés ou une mode, au lieu de développer son propre goût, et on voit clairement qu'un intérieur semble démodé, « dated » comme je le dis toujours. Il faut absolument tenter d'éviter cet écueil lorsqu'on sélectionne les maisons. Un autre critère de réussite est la diversité. Contempler une dixième maison avec le « bon » Damien Hirst au mur et les chaises Prouvé originales autour de la table est assommant pour le lecteur, alors qu'un objet fabriqué par les enfants avec du bois échoué met une touche de gaieté et de détente : c'est la variété qui crée l'ambiance.

J'accorde une importance particulière au choix des photos et à la manière dont elles se succèdent, car c'est la seule façon d'être sûr de créer une atmosphère capable de générer des émotions et de faire rêver. Il ne s'agit pas de montrer sagement une maison de A à Z, mais le fil conducteur doit rester perceptible, et la photo pleine page d'un rayon de lumière dans un verre d'eau fait quelquefois plus d'effet que la reproduction lisse d'un séjour parfaitement aménagé. Et évidemment il faut parler des photographes et de leur interprétation. Si vous faites photographier une maison par trois bons photographes, vous aurez l'impression de contempler trois intérieurs différents. Il faut donc choisir le photographe en fonction du style de la maison.

Même si, ces dernières années, des dizaines de tendances décoratives ont vu le jour et ont déjà disparu, la décoration des maisons en bord de mer est moins influencée par les modes qu'on serait en droit de s'y attendre à notre époque de mondialisation. À mon avis cela tient à ce que les gens ont la

mehr als ein Jahrzehnt auf dem Markt behaupten soll? Zunächst sollte es mit Kreativität, Entdeckungsfreude, Originalität und Liebe zum Detail eingerichtet sein – wobei völlig egal ist, ob der Hauseigentümer ein schwerreicher Kunstsammler ist, der einen weltweit tätigen Inneneinrichter beauftragt, oder ob das Haus einer jungen Familie ohne finanzielle Mittel gehört, die mit Fantasie alles selbst baut. Zehn Jahre nach Erscheinen des Buches oder einer Wohnzeitschrift kann man dann sehr gut beobachten, wer nur einem in den vielen Wohnzeitschriften propagierten Trends oder einer Mode gefolgt ist, anstatt einen eigenen Geschmack zu entwickeln. Dort sieht man deutlich, dass ein Interieur veraltet wirkt, wie ich immer sage, dass es „dated" aussieht. Dies sollte man bei der Auswahl der Häuser unbedingt versuchen zu vermeiden.

Ein weiteres Kriterium für das Gelingen eines Buches ist Abwechslungsreichtum. Das zehnte Haus mit dem „richtigen" Damien Hirst an der Wand und originalen Prouvé-Stühlen am Tisch langweilt bloß noch. Eine von Kindern selbst gebaute Treibholzskulptur dagegen lockert das Ganze auf. Eine Grundregel lautet also: Der Mix macht die Musik.

Besonders wichtig ist mir immer die Auswahl und Abfolge der Fotos, denn nur so kann in einem Buch eine Atmosphäre entstehen, die Emotionen erzeugt und zum Träumen anregt. Es geht nicht darum, ein Haus brav von A bis Z zu zeigen, der rote Faden muss allerdings spürbar bleiben, vielmehr kann das ganzseitige Foto eines Lichtstrahls in einem Wasserglas manchmal mehr Wirkung erzeugen als die korrekte Abbildung eines perfekt eingerichteten Wohnzimmers. Und natürlich muss man über die Fotografen und deren Interpretation reden. Wenn Sie ein Haus von drei guten Fotografen porträtieren lassen, haben Sie das Gefühl, drei völlig unterschiedliche Interieurs zu sehen, man muss also entscheiden, welcher Fotograf für welchen Einrichtungsstil am geeignetsten ist.

Auch wenn in den letzten Jahren Dutzende Wohntrends aufgekommen und wieder verschwunden sind: Die Inneneinrichtung von Häusern am Meer ist weniger von Moden beeinflusst, als man im Zeitalter der Globalisierung erwarten würde. Meines

an internet connection or even a television in their seaside homes. It's a way of ensuring that they really get a break from the everyday world.

One good development in recent years has been the growing tendency to employ first-class architects. It is the only way to guarantee lasting values. Good architecture has an immense influence on the psychological state of those who live in a house, and a well-proportioned room filled with light is quite simply a passport to happiness. If you have a view of the sea as well, you're practically in paradise.

I am particularly proud to be able to show the plain but magnificent house of Scandinavian architect Hanne Kjærholm in this book. She built it on the Danish coast back in 1959. It is one of the gems of modern architecture, and today serves as a wonderful setting for the celebrated furniture of her late husband, Poul. Every detail, from the pillars outside the terrace to the tea service and the lamps, is perfect, and without any sense of strain. The air of modesty, refinement and lightness is unrivalled. John Lautner's spectacular house in Acapulco, Mexico, makes an engaging contrast. But it doesn't have to be a famous architect. Another real dream house by the sea is a Dutchman's Robinson Crusoe idyll in Costa Rica (the mix is the thing!) – where everything, down to the smallest detail, was hand-made by the owner from whatever Nature offered.

I hope that as you turn the pages of this book you too will experience the magic of the sea.

nostalgie de la vie simple. On pêche le matin le poisson (ou on va le chercher au port) que l'on veut manger le midi. Le temps s'écoule à regarder la mer. De nombreux propriétaires rencontrés refusent d'installer Internet ou même la télévision pour pouvoir vraiment se déconnecter de leurs activités quotidiennes.

Une évolution positive de ces dernières années est que l'on a de plus en plus souvent recours à des architectes de premier ordre, les seuls capables de créer des valeurs sûres. L'architecture exerce une influence considérable sur le psychisme de l'habitant ; on se sent tout simplement heureux dans une pièce bien proportionnée et lumineuse, et si par bonheur la mer s'étend sous nos yeux, que souhaiter de plus ?

Je suis particulièrement fière de présenter ici la maison aussi simple que grandiose de l'architecte scandinave Hanne Kjærholm, un joyau de l'architecture moderne construit par ses soins dès 1959 sur la côte danoise et qui met aujourd'hui merveilleusement en valeur les célèbres meubles de son mari Poul aujourd'hui décédé. Tout ici est parfait, des détails des colonnes devant la terrasse au service à thé et aux lampes, et pourtant tout à fait relax. Il y règne une modestie, un raffinement et une légèreté inégalables.

La demeure spectaculaire de John Lautner à Acapulco au Mexique est le contraste tout trouvé. Mais nul besoin d'un architecte célèbre : le petit paradis à la Robinson Crusoé d'un Néerlandais au Costa Rica (vive la diversité !) est aussi un rêve concrétisé. Il a tout fait lui-même – et à la main – avec ce que la nature lui offrait.

J'espère qu'en feuilletant ces pages, vous serez vous aussi sensible à l'appel du large.

Erachtens liegt das an der Sehnsucht der Menschen nach einfachem Leben. Man fängt morgens den Fisch (oder holt ihn im Hafen), den man mittags essen möchte. Die Zeit verstreicht einfach beim Betrachten des Meeres. Viele der Hausbesitzer weigern sich, Internet oder auch nur Fernseher in ihren Häusern am Ozean zu haben, um wirklich eine Pause von ihrem Alltag machen zu können.

Eine andere Entwicklung der letzten Jahre ist, dass man immer häufiger auf erstklassige Architekten zurückgreift, denn nur so schafft man bleibende Werte. Gute Architektur hat einen immens großen Einfluss auf die Psyche des Bewohners, ein schön proportionierter Raum mit viel Licht ist einfach beglückend, wenn man dabei noch auf das Meer schauen kann, ist man fast schon im Paradies.

Besonders stolz bin ich, dass ich in diesem Buch das ebenso einfache wie großartige Haus der skandinavischen Architektin Hanne Kjærholm zeigen kann. Sie hat dieses Juwel moderner Architektur bereits 1959 an der dänischen Küste gebaut. Heute ist es ein wunderbarer Rahmen für die berühmten Möbel ihres verstorbenen Mannes Poul. Jedes Detail von den Säulen vor der Terrasse bis zum Teeservice und den Lampen ist perfekt, dabei völlig unverkrampft. Es herrscht eine Bescheidenheit, Feinheit und Leichtigkeit, die ihresgleichen sucht. Ein passender Kontrast dazu ist das spektakuläre Haus von John Lautner im mexikanischen Acapulco. Aber es muss nicht ein berühmter Architekt sein, ebenso ist beispielsweise die Robinson-Crusoe-Idylle eines Niederländers in Costa Rica (man muss mischen!) der Traum von einem Haus am Meer. Alles hand- und self-made bis ins kleinste Detail, aus dem was die Natur hergibt.

Ich hoffe, Sie werden beim Blättern in diesem Buch auch von der Magie des Meeres bezaubert.

Todd Saunders & Tommie Wilhelmsen

Hardanger, Norway

Quand Todd Saunders et Tommie Wilhelmsen ont ouvert leur cabinet d'architectes à Bergen, ils ne se sont pas mis en quête de clients mais d'un site où bâtir une maison expérimentale. Ils ont trouvé leur bonheur perché à 80 m au-dessus de l'un des fjords les plus spectaculaires de Norvège à Hardanger. Le bâtiment est aussi saisissant que la vue. Écologique, il est isolé avec du papier journal recyclé, n'a pas l'électricité et sa terrasse intègre les arbres existants. « Notre intention était de ne pas dénaturer les lieux », explique Saunders. « Quand la structure sera démolie dans 100 ou 200 ans, le paysage sera exactement le même. » En attendant, ils ont reçu commande de quatre autres cabanes et suscité l'intérêt des magazines du monde entier. « C'est un projet architecturel qui nous sert de carte visite plus grande que nature ».

When Todd Saunders and Tommie Wilhelmsen set up their architectural practice in Bergen, they didn't go looking for clients. They went hunting for a site on which to build a piece of experimental architecture. They found one perched 80 metres above one of Norway's most spectacular fjords, at Hardanger. The building itself is equally stunning. It is also ecological. Recycled newspapers were used for insulation, there is no electricity and the deck was built around existing trees. "The intent," states Saunders, "was not to put a scar on the land. When it's taken away in 100 or 200 years, the landscape will still be the same." In the meantime, it has led to commissions for four more cabanas and interest from magazines around the world. "It's a piece of architecture," says Saunders, "which acts as an extra-large business card."

Als Todd Saunders und Tommie Wilhelmsen ihr Architekturbüro in Bergen gründeten, hielten sie nicht gleich nach Auftraggebern Ausschau, sondern suchten stattdessen erst mal ein Grundstück, um darauf ein experimentelles Bauwerk zu errichten. Tatsächlich fanden sie ein geeignetes Stück Land, 80 Meter über einem der spektakulärsten Fjorde Norwegens in Hardanger gelegen. Das darauf errichtete Bauwerk ist ebenso fantastisch wie seine Lage und folgt darüber hinaus ökologischen Gesichtspunkten. Zur Isolierung diente Recyclingpapier, Elektrizität fehlt ganz, und die hölzerne Plattform wurde um die Bäume herum gebaut. Saunders erklärt: „Unser Ziel war es, der Natur keine Wunden zuzufügen. Wenn man das Häuschen in 100 oder 200 Jahren abreißt, bleibt die Landschaft unverändert zurück." Inzwischen hat das Häuschen Aufträge für vier weitere Hütten nach sich gezogen und das Interesse der Fachzeitschriften weltweit erregt. „Dieses Stück Architektur", meint Saunders, „dient uns als XXL-Visitenkarte."

Previous pages: The curvaceous larch-wood structure perches on the edge of an 80-square-metre deck made from fir.
Right and below: The cabana is situated just 80 metres from the dramatic Hardanger fjord. Its back wall is angled so that you can sit easily against it and admire the view.

Pages précédentes : La structure en mélèze aux angles arrondis est posée au bord d'une terrasse de 80 mètres carrés en sapin.
À droite et en bas : La cabane est perchée à 80 m au-dessus du spectaculaire fjord de Hardanger. Le mur du fond est incliné afin que l'on puisse s'y adosser pour admirer la vue.

Vorhergehende Seiten: Die kurvig geschwungene Struktur aus Lärchenholz ruht auf einer 80 Quadratmeter großen Plattform aus Kiefernholz, über deren Kante sie hinten hinausragt.
Rechts und unten: Die Hütte liegt knapp 80 Meter über dem dramatischen Hardanger Fjord. Ihre Rückwand ist sanft gerundet, sodass man sich an sie bequem anlehnen und die Aussicht bewundern kann.

Above: The interiors of the bedroom were deliberately kept simple.
The bed was made from fir wood by a friend of Saunders and
Wilhelmsen, the duvet and pillow covers are from Habitat and the
table from Ikea.
Right: The deck was built around the existing trees on the site.

En haut : Le décor de la chambre est délibérément dépouillé. Le lit
a été réalisé en sapin par un ami de Saunders et de Wilhelmsen. Le
duvet et la taie d'oreiller viennent de chez Habitat, la table basse de
chez Ikea.
À droite : La terrasse a été construite autour des arbres existants.

Oben: Die Inneneinrichtung des Schlafzimmers wurde bewusst
schlicht gehalten. Das Bett fertigte ein Freund der beiden Architekten
aus Kiefernholz an, Überzug und Kissenbezüge stammen von Habitat,
der Tisch von Ikea.
Rechts: Die Plattform wurde um die auf dem Grundstück vorhandenen
Bäume herum gebaut.

Hanne Kjærholm

Rungsted Kyst, Denmark

Hanne Kjærholm est l'une des plus éminentes architectes du Danemark. Son mari Poul, aujourd'hui disparu, fut l'un des plus grands créateurs de meubles du XXᵉ siècle. En 1959, le couple a acheté un terrain au bord du Øresund, le bras de mer entre le Danemark et la Suède. Hanne y a construit une maison de 4 chambres avec le chauffage par le sol (une nouveauté à l'époque) et un portique blanchi à la chaux « parce que l'horizon est tellement vaste qu'il risquait d'être écrasant ». Poul, lui, a aménagé l'intérieur en utilisant des matériaux naturels. Il y testait souvent ses prototypes avant de les mettre en production. Aujourd'hui, la maison reste une vitrine pour ses élégantes créations. Son endroit favori était le bureau dans l'immense pièce principale. « C'est là qu'on s'asseyait tous les deux face à face », se souvient Hanne.

Hanne Kjærholm is one of Denmark's most distinguished architects. Her late husband Poul was one of the 20th century's greatest furniture designers. In 1959, the couple bought a plot of land on the Øresund – the stretch of water between Denmark and Sweden. On it, Hanne built a four-bedroom house with underfloor heating (a novelty at the time) and a portico of whitewashed pillars. "I put in a portico because the horizon is so large, it could easily become overwhelming," she says. Poul, meanwhile, dealt with the interiors. He employed natural materials and would often test out new furniture designs before putting them into production. Today, the house still acts as a showcase for his elegant creations. His favourite spot, apparently, was the working desk in the immense main room. "It was there," recalls Hanne, "that we used to sit face-to-face."

Hanne Kjærholm ist eine der bedeutendsten Architektinnen Norwegens. Ihr verstorbener Gatte Poul gehörte zu den größten Möbeldesignern des 20. Jahrhunderts. 1959 kaufte das Paar ein Grundstück am Øresund, der Meerenge zwischen Dänemark und Schweden. Hier errichtete Hanne ein Haus mit vier Schlafzimmern und Fußbodenheizung (damals eine Neuheit) sowie einem Portikus mit weiß gestrichenen Säulen. „Ich habe einen Portikus hinzugefügt, weil der Horizont so weit ist, dass er einen leicht überwältigen könnte," sagt sie. Währenddessen befasste sich Poul mit der Inneneinrichtung. Dabei verwendete er natürliche Materialien und pflegte häufig neue Möbelentwürfe auszutesten, bevor er sie zur Produktion freigab. Heute fungiert das Haus immer noch als idealer Rahmen für seine eleganten Kreationen. Sein Lieblingsplatz war augenscheinlich sein Arbeitstisch in dem riesigen Hauptraum. „Hier saßen wir einander gewöhnlich gegenüber", erinnert sich Hanne.

Previous pages: A pair of "PK33" stools by Poul Kjærholm and custom-made steel and granite tables stand on the outdoor terrace, overlooking the Øresund strait.
Above: A view from the main living room of the terrace.
Right: Poul Kjærholm's "PK9" tulip chairs and a "PK54" table in the dining room. The painting is by Danish artist Arne Haugen Sørensen.
Facing page: A Grethe Meyer tea service on a table designed by Poul Kjærholm, which never went into production.

Pages précédentes : Sur la terrasse dominant le Øresund, une paire de tabourets « PK33 » de Poul Kjærholm et des tables basses en acier et granit réalisées sur mesure.
En haut : La terrasse vue du séjour.
À droite : Dans la salle à manger, des chaises tulipes « PK9 » et une table « PK54 » de Poul Kjærholm. Au mur, une œuvre de l'artiste danois Arne Haugen Sørensen.
Page de droite : Un service à thé de Grethe Meyer sur une table dessinée par Poul Kjærholm mais jamais commercialisée.

Vorhergehende Seiten: Zwei „PK33"-Hocker von Poul Kjærholm und aus Stahl und Granit maßgefertigte Tische stehen auf der Außenterrasse mit Aussicht auf den Øresund.
Oben: Blick vom großen Wohnzimmer auf die Terrasse.
Rechts: Poul Kjærholms Tulip Chairs „PK9" und ein „PK54"-Tisch im Esszimmer. Das Gemälde ist ein Werk des dänischen Malers Arne Haugen Sørensen.
Gegenüberliegende Seite: Ein Grethe-Meyer-Teeservice auf einem von Poul Kjærholm entworfenen Tisch, der jedoch nie in Produktion ging.

New Seaside Interiors   Hanne Kjærholm

Facing page: Sisal flooring made in Haiti is used in the hallway, as elsewhere in the house.
Above: Pine panelling and white-washed bricks were used for the walls in the dining room.
Right: A work by Arne Haugen Sørensen hangs above a black, painted plywood "PKo" chair in the entrance hall.

Page de gauche : Dans le couloir comme dans le reste de la maison, un revêtement de sol en sisal réalisé à Haïti.
En haut : Dans la salle à manger, les murs sont lambrissés de pin ou en briques blanchies à la chaux.
À droite : Dans l'entrée, une œuvre d'Arne Haugen Sørensen au-dessus d'un siège « PKo » en contreplaqué peint en noir.

Gegenüberliegende Seite: Der in Haiti hergestellte Sisal-Bodenbelag wurde nicht nur für den Eingangsbereich und Flur, sondern auch für die übrigen Räume im Haus verwendet.
Oben: Vertäfelungen aus Kiefernholz und weiß getünchte Ziegelsteine wurden für die Wände im Esszimmer eingesetzt.
Rechts: Im Eingangsbereich hängt ein Werk von Arne Haugen Sørensen über einem schwarz lackierten „PKo"-Stuhl aus Sperrholz.

Right: Two portraits of Poul Kjærholm and a model for a make-up box designed by Hanne; a "PK41" folding stool stands in front of the "PK111" screen made from Oregon pine.
Below: The main room on the ground floor is home to the lounge, dining room and office. Here, two "PK31/2" sofas stand on a Moroccan rug. The standing light is the "Bestlite BL3" model by Robert Dudley Best.

À droite : Deux portraits de Poul Kjærholm et la maquette d'un coffret à maquillage réalisé par Hanne ; un tabouret pliant « PK41 » devant un paravent « PK111 » en pin de l'Oregon.
En bas : La grande pièce principale au rez-de-chaussée fait office de salon, de salle à manger et de bureau. Sur un tapis marocain, deux canapés « PK31/2 ». Le lampadaire « Bestlite BL3 » est de Robert Dudley Best.

Rechts: Zwei Porträts von Poul Kjærholm sowie der von Hanne entworfene Prototyp einer Make-up-Box; ein „PK41"-Klappsitz vor dem „PK111"-Wandschirm aus Douglastanne.
Unten: Der Hauptwohnbereich im Erdgeschoss enthält Wohnzimmer, Esszimmer und Arbeitszimmer. Hier stehen zwei „PK31/2"-Sofas auf einem marokkanischen Teppich. Die Stehlampe ist das Modell „Bestlite BL3" von Robert Dudley Best.

Above: The work table at which the Kjærholms used to sit opposite each other. The vintage ceiling light was designed by Poul Henningsen and the bookshelves by Mogens Koch.
Right: The bedspread in Hanne's room was made in Mexico.
Following pages: On the left is perhaps Poul Kjærholm's most iconic piece – the "PK24" rattan chaise longue, which dates from 1965.

En haut : Le bureau où les Kjærholm travaillaient face à face. Le plafonnier a été dessiné par Poul Henningsen et la bibliothèque par Mogens Koch.
À droite : Le dessus-de-lit dans la chambre de Hanne vient du Mexique.
Double page suivante : À gauche, la chaise longue en rotin « PK24 », sans doute la pièce la plus célèbre de Poul Kjærholm. Il l'a créée en 1965.

Oben: Der Arbeitstisch, an dem die Kjærholms einander gegenübersaßen. Die Vintage-Deckenleuchte wurde von Poul Henningsen entworfen, die Bücherregale stammen von Mogens Koch.
Rechts: Der Bettüberwurf in Hannes Zimmer ist eine Handarbeit aus Mexiko.
Folgende Seiten: Links ist das Möbelstück zu sehen, das vielleicht den größten Kultstatus hat – der „PK24"-Rattan-Liegestuhl aus dem Jahr 1965.

Black Rubber
Beach House

Dungeness Beach, England

Les maisons de vacances de Dungeness Beach sont un drôle de
méli-mélo, incluant des cottages enduits de goudron et des wagons
désaffectés. Comme le dit l'architecte londonien Simon Conder : « Elles
ont toutes un côté improvisé. » Appelé pour convertir cette cabane
de pêcheur des années 30, il a fini par la transformer complètement,
l'étendant pour créer une terrasse et un séjour d'été, faisant saillir
une salle de bains d'un côté et recyclant l'ancien abri à outils en hall
d'entrée. Il a également recouvert le tout d'un revêtement en caoutchouc noir comme on en utilise pour les tapis roulants. La structure
ne comptant qu'une petite chambre, les propriétaires ont garé une
caravane Airstream de 1954 à côté pour y accueillir les amis. Conder
est ravi du résultat : « Les réactions sont extraordinaires. Les touristes
font le détour pour venir voir la maison. »

The holiday homes at Dungeness Beach are something of a mish-
mash. Among other things, there are black tar-painted cottages and
old railway carriages. "Every structure has an improvised nature,"
asserts London-based architect Simon Conder. This house started
out life as a 1930s fisherman's hut. Initially called in to convert it,
Conder ended up completely transforming it. He extended it to create a deck and summer living room. He cantilevered a bathroom
off one side and made an entrance hall out of a former garden
shed. He also clad the whole structure in the sort of black rubber
normally used for conveyor belts. Inside is only one small bedroom.
So, the owners parked a 1954 Airstream caravan next door to act as
guest accommodation. "The reactions have been extraordinary,"
enthuses Conder. "The house has become something of a tourist
destination."

Die Ferienhäuser an der Dungeness Beach stellen eine merkwürdig
bunte Mischung dar. Es gibt mit Teer schwarz gestrichene Hütten,
aber auch alte Eisenbahnwaggons. „Jedes Bauwerk hat einen impro-
visierten Charakter", erklärt der Londoner Architekt Simon Conder.
Das hier gezeigte Haus begann sein Leben in den 1930er-Jahren als
Fischerhütte. Conder war ursprünglich damit beauftragt, es nur ein
wenig umzubauen, am Ende aber veränderte er es völlig. Er erweiterte
es um eine Veranda und einen Wohnbereich für den Sommer, fügte
seitlich ein Badezimmer an und schuf aus einem ehemaligen Schuppen im Garten den Eingangsbereich. Dann verkleidete er das ganze
Bauwerk mit jenem schwarzen Gummi, aus dem normalerweise
Fließbänder gemacht werden. Da es nur ein kleines Schlafzimmer
gibt, parkten die Eigentümer einen amerikanischen Caravan von 1954
als Gästezimmer neben dem Haus. „Die Reaktionen waren außerge-
wöhnlich", schwärmt Conder. „Der Bau ist zu einer Art Touristen-
attraktion geworden."

Previous pages: *A former shed was turned into an entrance hall and linked to the main body of the house with a glass collar.*
Right: *Officially called "Vista", the house has earned more than a dozen prizes and been shortlisted for the Mies van der Rohe Award.*
Below: *The aluminium of the 1954 Airstream Globe Trotter caravan contrasts with the black rubber cladding of the house.*

Pages précédentes : *L'ancien abri a été transformé en vestibule et relié au reste de la maison par un sas en verre.*
À droite : *Baptisée « Vista », la maison a remporté plus d'une douzaine de prix et été sélectionnée pour le Mies van der Rohe Award.*
En bas : *L'aluminium de la caravane Airstream Globe-Trotter 1954 contraste avec le caoutchouc noir de la maison.*

Vorhergehende Seiten: *Ein mit dem Haupthaus durch einen gläsernen Korridor verbundener ehemaliger Schuppen wurde zur Eingangshalle.*
Rechts: *Das Haus mit dem offiziellen Namen „Vista" hat über ein Dutzend Preise gewonnen und wurde auch für den Mies-van-der-Rohe-Preis nominiert.*
Unten: *Das Aluminium des 1954er Airstream Globe Trotter Caravans kontrastiert mit der schwarzen Gummiverkleidung des Hauses.*

Above: Architect Simon Conder extended the house to the south and east to create a summer living room and deck.
Right: The interior was clad with Wisa Spruce plywood from a managed forest in Finland. The owners – a solicitor and an actress – have placed a grand piano in the winter living room.

En haut : L'architecte Simon Conder a étendu la maison vers le sud et l'est pour créer un séjour d'été et une terrasse.
À droite : L'intérieur est tapissé en contreplaqué d'épicéa Wisa-Spruce provenant d'une forêt gérée en Finlande. Les propriétaires, un avocat et une actrice, ont placé leur piano à queue dans le séjour d'hiver.

Oben: Der Architekt Simon Conder erweiterte das Haus nach Süden und Osten, um einen Wohnbereich für den Sommer mit davor liegender Terrasse zu schaffen.
Rechts: Das Interieur wurde mit „Wisa-Spruce"-Sperrholz aus einem industriell bewirtschafteten Forst in Finnland verkleidet. Die Eigentümer – ein Anwalt und eine Schauspielerin – haben einen großen Flügel ins Winter-Wohnzimmer gestellt.

Facing page: A bent plywood chair found at Camden Passage Market and a Robin Day sideboard in the winter living room.
Above: The two red chairs and the glass and beech coffee table in the summer living room were bought in vintage furniture stores in London.
Right: A Robin Day table and chairs in the kitchen.
Following pages: The caravan acts as accommodation for guests. The owners brought back the 1950s fabrics from Los Angeles.

Page de gauche : Dans le séjour d'hiver, un fauteuil en contreplaqué trouvé au Camden Passage Market et une crédence de Robin Day.
En haut : Les deux fauteuils rouges et la table basse en hêtre et verre du séjour d'été ont été achetés à Londres chez des antiquaires spécialisés dans le mobilier vintage.
À droite : Dans la cuisine, une table et des chaises de Robin Day.
Pages suivantes : La caravane sert de chambre d'amis. Les propriétaires ont apporté les tissus des années 50 de Los Angeles.

Gegenüberliegende Seite: Der Sessel aus formgebogenem Sperrholz im Winter-Wohnzimmer wurde im Camden Passage Market gekauft; an der Wand steht ein Robin-Day-Sideboard.
Oben: Die beiden roten Stühle und der Beistelltisch aus Glas und Buchenholz im Sommer-Wohnbereich stammen aus Londoner Vintage-Möbelgeschäften.
Rechts: Ein Robin-Day-Tisch samt Stühlen in der Küche.
Folgende Seiten: Der Caravan fungiert als Gästezimmer. Die Stoffe mit den typischen Mustern der 1950er-Jahre brachten die Hauseigentümer aus Los Angeles mit.

Seaside Simplicity
Knokke-Zoute, Belgium

Le Zwynelande, un immeuble à Knokke-le-Zoute datant de la fin des années 60, est pris en sandwich entre la mer et une réserve naturelle que les Belges ont baptisée le Zwin. « C'est comme un désert, très calme et reposant », s'émerveille l'architecte Vincent Van Duysen. Il s'est chargé de rénover un appartement avec trois chambres particulièrement délabré qui appartenait autrefois à une dame de 93 ans, cherchant à ouvrir l'espace et à profiter au maximum des vues. « À mon réveil, je voulais pouvoir contempler la mer et les dunes du Zwin », explique le propriétaire. Van Duysen a donc abattu des murs et utilisé les mêmes matériaux dans tout l'espace pour créer une impression de continuité. Dans la chambre principale, notamment, la baignoire s'étire jusqu'auprès du lit pour former une table de chevet.

The Zwynelande apartment building in Knokke-Zoute is sandwiched between the sea and a dune landscape, which the Belgians call Zwin. "It's like a desert. It's very calm and restful," enthuses architect Vincent Van Duysen, who oversaw the renovation of this three-bedroom apartment. Dating from the late 1960s, it previously belonged to a 93-year-old woman and was completely rundown. Van Duysen's goal was to open up both the space and views as much as possible. "I wanted to wake up and be able to see both the sea and Zwin," explains the owner. To this end, Van Duysen knocked down a maximum number of walls and used the same materials throughout to create a sense of continuity. In the master suite, there is certainly something of an overlap. In a nice touch, the bath surround extends and doubles up as a bedside table.

Das Zwynelande-Apartmenthaus in Knokke-Zoute liegt zwischen dem Meer und einer von den Belgiern „Zwin" (und von den Deutschen „Swin") genannten Dünenlandschaft. „Sie ist wie eine Wüste. Sehr ruhig und entspannend", schwärmt der Architekt Vincent Van Duysen, der für die Renovierung dieses Apartments mit drei Schlafzimmern verantwortlich war. In den späten 1960er-Jahren gebaut, gehörte es zuvor einer 93-jährigen Dame und war vollkommen heruntergekommen. Van Duysens Ziel war es, sowohl den Wohnraum als auch die Ausblicke so weit wie möglich zu öffnen. „Ich wollte beim Aufwachen sowohl das Meer als auch den Zwin sehen", erklärt der Besitzer. Zu diesem Zweck riss Van Duysen so viele Trennwände wie irgend möglich nieder und verwendete durchweg dieselben Materialien, um ein Gefühl der Kontinuität zu erzeugen. Auf diese Weise ergaben sich auch im Hauptschlafzimmer fließende Übergänge, etwa durch die Idee, die Wannenumrandung in ihrer Verlängerung als Nachttisch zu nutzen.

Previous pages: A pair of "Butterfly" chairs on the balcony overlooking the sea. At the rear of the building is the dune landscape, which the Belgians call Zwin.
Above: A pair of "Greta" armchairs designed by Antonio Citterio stands on a vintage Iranian wool carpet in the living room. The owners use the telescope to observe both boats and kites.
Right: An abstract oil painting by Jason Martin hangs above Antonio Citterio's "Groundpiece" sofa for Flexform. The two white coffee tables were designed by Ronan & Erwan Bouroullec.

Pages précédentes : Sur le balcon dominant la mer, une paire de sièges « Butterfly ». L'arrière du bâtiment donne sur le Zwin, un paysage de dunes.
En haut : Dans le séjour, une paire de fauteuils « Greta » d'Antonio Citterio sur un tapis en laine iranien ancien. Le télescope sert aux propriétaires pour observer les bateaux et les cerfs-volants.
À droite : Une toile abstraite de Jason Martin au-dessus d'un canapé dessiné par Antonio Citterio pour Flexform. Les deux tables basses blanches sont de Ronan & Erwan Bouroullec.

Vorhergehende Seiten: Auf dem Balkon mit Meerblick stehen zwei „Butterfly"-Sessel. Hinter dem Gebäude liegt die von den Belgiern „Zwin" genannte Dünenlandschaft.
Oben: Zwei von Antonio Citterio entworfene „Greta"-Lehnsessel stehen im Wohnzimmer auf einem antiken iranischen Wollteppich mit geometrischem Muster. Die Besitzer benutzen das Teleskop, um die Schiffe und Drachenflieger zu beobachten.
Rechts: Ein abstraktes Ölgemälde von Jason Martin hängt über Antonio Citterios für Flexform geschaffenem „Groundpiece"-Sofa. Die beiden weißen Beistelltischchen sind Entwürfe von Ronan & Erwan Bouroullec.

Right: The glass mosaic bath surround doubles as a bedside table. The wooden sculpture is from Botswana.
Below: The kitchen is the "Tile" model, which Vincent Van Duysen created for Obumex. Bertoia Side Chairs are grouped around an Eero Saarinen dining table.

À droite : Le rebord en mosaïque de verre de la baignoire s'étire jusque dans la chambre pour devenir table de chevet. La sculpture en bois vient du Botswana.
En bas : La cuisine est équipée d'éléments « Tile » que Van Duysen a créés pour Obumex. Des chaises de Bertoia sont regroupées autour d'une table d'Eero Saarinen.

Rechts: Die Badewannenumrandung aus Mosaikglassteinen verwandelt sich in ihrer Verlängerung in einen Nachttisch. Die Holzskulptur stammt aus Botswana.
Unten: Die Küche ist das von Vincent Van Duysen für Obumex entworfene Modell „Tile". Bertoia-Stühle sind um einen Esstisch von Eero Saarinen gruppiert.

Pierre Cardin
Saint-Tropez, France

Le cocon flottant de Pierre Cardin, Anthénéa, doit son nom au mot grec pour « éclosion ». Son design a été inspiré par la scène finale de « L'Espion qui m'aimait », où James Bond s'échappait avec la belle à bord d'une capsule amphibie. Son concepteur, l'architecte Jean-Michel Ducancelle, l'a réalisé en fibre de verre et équipé d'un fond transparent pour admirer la faune marine. « C'est très relaxant. On a la sensation de flotter sur l'eau », affirme-t-il. Il est également plus stable qu'un bateau et « peut résister à un cyclone ». Cardin l'a décoré dans le pur style des années 70, avec des tissus graphiques noirs et blancs. Il existe une version plus grande avec jacuzzi, un système hi-fi Bang & Olufsen et une connexion Internet sans fil. « Il y a plein de gadgets pour se mettre à la place de James Bond », confie Ducancelle.

The name of Pierre Cardin's floating habitat – "Anthénéa" – is derived from the Greek word for blossom. Its design was inspired by the final scene of *The Spy Who Loved Me*, in which James Bond escapes with his lover in a sea capsule. The brainwave of French architect Jean-Michel Ducancelle, it is made from fibreglass and has a glass bottom, which allows you to admire marine life close-up. "It's very relaxing," says Ducancelle. "You feel like you're actually floating in the water." It's also more stable than a boat. "It can resist a cyclone," he adds. Cardin has fitted his capsule out in the pure 1970s style, with black-and-white fabrics. A larger version has a built-in Jacuzzi, as well as a Bang & Olufsen hi-fi system and wireless Internet hook-ups. "There are lots of gadgets," states Ducancelle. "That way, you can really play at being James Bond."

Der Name von Pierre Cardins schwimmendem Wohnobjekt – „Anthénéa" – ist von dem griechischen Wort für „Blüte" abgeleitet. Und dessen Entwurf ist von der letzten Szene des Films „Der Spion, der mich liebte" inspiriert, in der sich James Bond samt Gespielin in einer wasserdichten Kapsel an Land rettet. Die Idee zu der Seekapsel stammt von dem französischen Architekten Jean-Michel Ducancelle. Sie besteht aus Fiberglas und hat einen Glasboden, durch den man das Leben unter Wasser aus nächster Nähe beobachten kann. „Das ist ebenso entspannend", sagt Ducancelle, „als wäre man selbst im Wasser." Die Kapsel ist stabiler als ein Schiff. „Sie kann einem Zyklon trotzen", fügt er hinzu. Cardin hat sie im Stil der 1970er-Jahre ganz in kontrastierendem Schwarz-Weiß eingerichtet. Die größere Variante hat einen eingebauten Whirlpool sowie eine Hi-Fi-Anlage von Bang & Olufsen und einen drahtlosen Internet-Anschluss. „Mit diesem technischen Equipment", meint Ducancelle, „kann man selbst James Bond spielen."

Previous page: The main fibreglass door is opened by means of a hydraulic jack.
Above: Cardin owns the smallest version of the "Anthénéa", which measures 4.60 metres in diameter. Inventor Jean-Michel Ducancelle's aim is to create floating holiday resorts, consisting of several capsules linked by bridges.
Right: Verner Panton's "Fun" table lamp, made from mother of pearl.

Page précédente : La porte principale en fibre de verre s'ouvre à l'aide d'un vérin hydraulique.
En haut : Cardin possède la version la plus petite de l'Anthénéa, qui mesure 4,60 m de diamètre. L'objectif de son inventeur, Jean-Michel Ducancelle, est de créer des villages de vacances flottants avec plusieurs capsules reliées par des passerelles.
À droite : La lampe « Fun » de Verner Panton, réalisée en nacre.

Vorhergehende Seite: Die Haupteingangstür aus Fiberglas lässt sich durch eine hydraulische Hebevorrichtung öffnen.
Oben: Cardin besitzt die kleinste Variante der „Anthénéa" mit einem Durchmesser von 4,60 Metern. Jean-Michel Ducancelle, ihr Erfinder, plant eine Anlage schwimmender Ferienhotels, die aus mehreren durch Brücken verbundenen Kapseln besteht.
Rechts: Verner Pantons „Fun"-Tischlampe aus Perlmutt.

Right: *Cardin opted to used black and white optical fabrics throughout the interior.*
Below: *An anchor-like sculpture stands on a maple-veneer table, which can be lowered into the floor.*

À droite : *Pour l'intérieur, Cardin a opté pour des tissus imprimés de motifs noirs et blancs créant des illusions d'optique.*
En bas : *Une sculpture en forme d'ancre sur une table plaquée en érable qui peut descendre au ras du sol.*

Rechts: *Cardin entschied sich bei der gesamten Inneneinrichtung für Stoffe in kontrastierendem Schwarz-Weiß.*
Unten: *Eine Skulptur, die an einen Anker erinnert, steht auf einem im Boden versenkbaren Tisch mit Ahornfurnier.*

Marcella & Gianpietro Vigorelli

Levanto, Italy

La station balnéaire de Levanto en Ligurie est surnommée « la porte des Cinque Terre ». Elle est connue pour son château du XIIᵉ siècle et la Villa Agnelli. Elle compte également une autre grande demeure qui abrite l'appartement du publicitaire milanais Gianpietro Vigorelli et de son épouse Marcella. Le bâtiment de style mauresque date du début du XXᵉ siècle. À l'intérieur, le couple a associé à l'architecture traditionnelle des classiques du design contemporain, respectant la palette des rouges, des ocres et des verts pâles des façades de Levanto. Adorant la mer et la pêche, Vigorelli possède un bateau à moteur et loue un yacht chaque été. « Je suis un vrai Milanais », confie-t-il. « Il n'y a pas de marin plus passionné que ceux nés loin de la mer ».

The Ligurian resort of Levanto is known as "the doorway to the Cinque Terre." It is also renowned for its 12th-century castle and the Villa Agnelli. On the opposite side of town is another grand dwelling, which is home to the apartment of Milanese advertising executive Gianpietro Vigorelli and his wife Marcella. The building dates from the early 20th century and was constructed in the Moorish style. Inside, the couple respected that architectural traditional and mixed in modern design classics. They also worked with the same palette of reds, ochres and light greens found on the façades of Levanto's houses. Vigorelli admits to having a passion for the sea. He loves fishing, owns a motorboat and rents a yacht each summer. "I'm a true Milanese," he says. "I don't think there are more passionate sailors than those born far from the sea."

Der ligurische Badeort Levanto gilt als Tor zur Region „Cinque Terre". Ein Kastell aus dem 12. Jahrhundert und die Villa Agnelli tragen zu seiner Berühmtheit bei. Auf der anderen Seite des Ortes befindet sich in einer großen Villa das Apartment des Mailänder Werbemanagers Gianpietro Vigorelli und seiner Frau Marcella. Das Gebäude wurde Anfang des 20. Jahrhunderts im maurischen Stil erbaut. Im Inneren respektierte das Paar dieses überlieferte architektonische Umfeld, kombinierte es aber mit modernen Design-Klassikern. Dabei fand dieselbe Palette von Rottönen, Ocker und hellem Grün Anwendung, wie sie auch auf den Fassaden der Häuser von Levanto zu finden ist. Vigorelli liebt das Meer. Er ist ein begeisterter Fischer, besitzt ein Motorboot und mietet jeden Sommer eine Jacht. „Ich bin ein echter Mailänder", sagt er. „Ich glaube, es gibt keine leidenschaftlicheren Seefahrer als uns Landratten."

Previous pages: The façade of the house, with its elaborate painted motifs, is typical of the Moorish style. The rattan chair on the loggia was bought in Forte dei Marmi.
Above: The dining chairs are Arne Jacobsen's Series 7 model.
Right: Several items by Smeg are integrated into the kitchen.

Pages précédentes : La façade, peinte de motifs complexes, est typique du style mauresque. Le fauteuil en rotin sur la loggia a été acheté à Forte dei Marmi.
En haut : Dans la salle à manger, des chaises de la Série 7 d'Arne Jacobsen.
À droite : La cuisine, équipée d'électroménager de chez Smeg.

Vorhergehende Seiten: Die Hausfassade mit ihren kunstvoll aufge-malten Motiven ist typisch für den maurischen Stil. Der Rattan-Stuhl in der Loggia wurde in Forte dei Marmi gekauft.
Oben: Die Esstischstühle sind Modelle der 7er-Serie von Arne Jacobsen. Sie stehen um einen Tisch von Bruno Mathson und Piet Hein.
Rechts: In die Küche wurden Geräte von Smeg integriert.

Right: Gianpietro Vigorelli designed the twin beds in the guestroom himself. The bedside tables are Chinese antiques.
Below: The living room is decorated with a De Padova sofa, Arne Jacobsen's "Egg" chair, Harry Bertoia's "Bird" lounge chair and ottoman and a Moroccan rug.

À droite : Gianpietro Vigorelli a dessiné lui-même les lits jumeaux de la chambre d'amis. Les tables de chevet anciennes sont chinoises.
En bas : Dans le séjour, un canapé de De Padova, un fauteuil « Egg » d'Arne Jacobsen, un fauteuil et repose-pied « Bird » d'Harry Bertoia et un tapis marocain.

Rechts: Die beiden Betten für das Gästezimmer hat Gianpietro Vigorelli eigenhändig entworfen, die Nachttische sind chinesische Antiquitäten.
Unten: Das Wohnzimmer ist mit einem Sofa von De Padova, Arne Jacobsens „Egg"-Sessel, Harry Bertoias „Bird"-Sessel samt Ottomane sowie einem marokkanischen Teppich eingerichtet.

Kris Ruhs
Portofino, Italy

« Tout l'intérêt est dans la vue », déclare l'artiste américain Kris Ruhs. « Quand on entre, on va droit à la fenêtre. » L'endroit en question est une maison du début du XXᵉ siècle haut perchée au-dessus de la mer à Portofino. Un sentier sinueux descend vers le jardin et une plage privée. Quand Ruhs l'a vue la première fois, elle était abandonnée depuis 20 ans. « La terrasse était envahie de plantes sauvages. » À l'intérieur, il a opté pour un décor principalement noir et blanc « Avec tout le bleu de la mer, inutile d'ajouter de la couleur. » Il a créé un séjour ouvert meublé de classiques du design des années 60 et 70, ainsi que de ses propres créations. À l'étage inférieur, la paroi rocheuse laissée exposée rappelle une grotte. Pour Ruhs, sa propriété offre « le meilleur de deux mondes. Elle est très privée mais on est dans le port en deux secondes. »

"The whole place is about the view," declares American artist Kris Ruhs. "When you enter, you head straight for the window." The "place" in question is an early 20th-century house, perched right on the sea at Portofino. A winding path leads down to a garden and a private beach. When Ruhs first set eyes on it, the house had been abandoned for 20 years. "The terrace was overgrown and very wild," he recalls. Inside, he opened up the living room and opted for a largely black-and-white décor. "You have all the blue of the sea. So, you don't need to add colour," he opines. He integrated design classics from the 1960s and 1970s, as well as many of his own creations. Downstairs, the exposed rock walls are reminiscent of a cave. For Ruhs, the property offers "the best of both worlds". "It's very private," he states. "Yet, in two seconds, you're at the port."

„Bei diesem ganzen Ort hier geht es nur um die Aussicht", erklärt der amerikanische Künstler Kris Ruhs. „Beim Eintreten zieht es einen sofort ans Fenster." Der „Ort" ist ein Haus aus dem frühen 20. Jahrhundert, das sich über dem Meer auf der Felsenküste von Portofino erhebt. Ein kleiner Hohlweg führt hinab zum Garten und an einen privaten Strand. Als Ruhs das Haus zum ersten Mal sah, hatte es 20 Jahre lang leer gestanden. „Die Terrasse war überwuchert und verwildert", erinnert er sich. Im Hausinneren wählte er eine offene Raumgestaltung für das Wohnzimmer und ein größtenteils schwarz-weißes Dekor. „Es gibt ja das ganze Blau des Meeres. Man muss also keine Farben hinzufügen", meint er. Er integrierte Design-Klassiker aus den 1960er- und 1970er-Jahren sowie viele seiner eigenen Kreationen. Unten im Haus erinnern die freigelegten Felswände an eine Höhle. Für Ruhs bietet das Anwesen „das Beste aus zwei Welten". „Es ist sehr abgeschieden", sagt er, „aber man ist in zwei Sekunden am Hafen."

Below: *Ruhs initially created the raku stools for the Milan Furniture Fair.*
Facing page: *A view from the entrance into the main room. The two curvaceous steel standing lamps were also designed by the owner.*

En bas : *Ruhs a créé ces tabourets en raku pour la foire du meuble de Milan.*
Page de droite : *La salle principale vue de l'entrée. Les deux lampadaires en acier aux formes arrondies sont des créations du maître de maison.*

Unten: *Die Hocker aus Raku-Keramik hatte Ruhs ursprünglich für die Mailänder Möbelmesse geschaffen.*
Gegenüberliegende Seite: *Blick vom Eingang in den zentralen Wohnbereich. Die beiden stählernen Stehlampen mit den schwingenden Formen wurden ebenfalls vom Hauseigentümer entworfen.*

Previous pages: *The house hugs the rocky coastline of Portofino.*
Above: *On the terrace are Harry Bertoia chairs and a steel and ceramic table created by Ruhs.*

Pages précédentes : *La maison accrochée à la falaise sur la côte de Portofino.*
En haut : *Sur la terrasse, des fauteuils d'Harry Bertoia et une table en acier et céramique de Ruhs.*

Vorhergehende Seiten: *Das Haus liegt auf der felsigen Küste von Portofino.*
Oben: *Auf der Terrasse stehen Harry-Bertoia-Stühle und ein von Ruhs selbst gestalteter Tisch aus Stahl und Keramik.*

New Seaside Interiors   Kris Ruhs

Above: *Two white seats by Roberto Sebastian Matta in front of the resin kitchen bar. The artworks are oils on paper by Ruhs.*
Right: *A Serge Mouille sconce protrudes over the Arne Jacobsen dining table and chairs; a Pierre Paulin sofa wraps its way around the walls of the sitting room.*

En haut : *Deux fauteuils blancs de Roberto Sebastian Matta devant le comptoir de la cuisine. Au murs, des huiles sur papier de Ruhs.*
À droite : *Une applique de Serge Mouille s'avance au-dessus d'une table et des chaises d'Arne Jacobsen. Le canapé de Pierre Paulin épouse les formes courbes du salon.*

Oben: *Zwei weiße Sessel von Roberto Sebastian Matta vor der schwarzen Küchentheke. Die Bilder sind Ölgemälde auf Papier von Ruhs.*
Rechts: *Die Arme eines Wandleuchters von Serge Mouille ragen über den Arne-Jacobsen-Esstisch mit seinen Stühlen; ein Pierre-Paulin-Sofa zieht sich an den Wänden des Wohnzimmers entlang.*

New Seaside Interiors   Kris Ruhs

Right: Pierre Paulin's "Mushroom" chair and ottoman are paired with Serge Mouille standing lights in the bedroom.
Below: The lower level was carved directly out of the rock face. The geometric bed linens were designed by Nigel Atkinson.

À droite : Dans la chambre, un fauteuil et un pouf « Mushroom » de Pierre Paulin près de deux lampadaires de Serge Mouille.
En bas : Le niveau inférieur a été creusé dans la falaise. Le dessus-de-lit aux motifs géométriques a été dessiné par Nigel Atkinson.

Rechts: Pierre Paulins „Mushroom Chair" und Ottomane mit Serge-Mouille-Stehlampen im Schlafzimmer.
Unten: Die untere Wohnebene wurde direkt aus dem Felsgestein geschlagen. Die Bettbezüge mit dem geometrischen Muster sind ein Entwurf von Nigel Atkinson.

Domenico Dolce & Stefano Gabbana

Portofino, Italy

Même si Silvio Berlusconi l'a loué 15 étés de suite, au moment de s'en séparer, l'ancienne propriétaire de ce domaine de six hectares, une comtesse génoise, a décidé qu'elle ne pouvait le confier qu'à Domenico Dolce et Stefano Gabbana. Dominant la sublime baie de Portofino, le terrain accueille plusieurs structures indépendantes, si bien que chacun a sa villa et sa maison d'amis. Le deux stylistes les ont toutes réaménagées avec l'aide de l'architecte Ferruccio Laviani, tandis que les jardins « en friche » ont été redessinés par Giorgio Fornari. Dolce décrit sa Villa Bianca comme « un conte de fées, un peu Disneyland, un peu Cendrillon », alors que la Villa Olivetta de Gabbana est un mélange capiteux. On trouve ici des murs tapissés de pivoines géantes, une cuisine revêtue de mosaïque en miroirs et céramiques siciliennes et un canapé recouvert de 70 peaux d'ocelot !

Silvio Berlusconi may have rented the property for 15 summers, but when it came to selling it, the former owner (a Genoese countess) decreed that the only people she'd trust to own it were design duo Domenico Dolce and Stefano Gabbana. Situated on the stunning bay of Portofino, the six hectares of land are home to a number of independent structures. Both designers have their own villa and their own guesthouse. On all of them, they worked with architect Ferruccio Laviani, while the "wild, abandoned" gardens, were re-landscaped by Giorgio Fornari. Dolce says his Villa Bianca is "like a fairytale, like Disney World, like Cinderella". As for Gabbana's Villa Olivetta, it is a heady mix. There are walls covered in an oversized peony print, a kitchen clad in a mosaic of Sicilian pottery and mirrors, and a sofa upholstered in some 70 ocelot skins!

Silvio Berlusconi mag das Anwesen ja 15 Sommer lang gemietet haben. Doch als es um den Verkauf ging, erklärte die vormalige Besitzerin (eine genuesische Gräfin), dass sie es einzig dem Designer-Duo Domenico Dolce und Stefano Gabbana als Eigentümern anvertrauen würde. Das an der überwältigenden Bucht von Portofino gelegene und sechs Hektar umfassende Grundstück ist mit etlichen, voneinander unabhängigen Gebäuden bebaut. Beide Designer haben hier jeweils ihre eigene Villa und ihr eigenes Gästehaus. Bei allen Gebäuden arbeiteten sie mit dem Designer Ferruccio Laviani zusammen, während die „verwilderten, verlassenen" Gärten von Giorgio Fornari landschaftlich neu gestaltet wurden. Dolce meint, die Atmosphäre seiner Villa Bianca sei mit „einem Märchen, Disney World, Cinderella" vergleichbar. Gabbanas Villa Olivetta dagegen bietet eine verwirrend opulente Mischung an Stilen. Da gibt es mit riesigen Päonien-Mustern tapezierte Wände, eine mit sizilianischen Keramik- und Spiegel-Mosaiken ausgekleidete Küche und ein mit etwa 70 Ozelotfellen bezogenes Sofa.

Previous page: Sun-beds are arranged on the terrace of Stefano Gabbana's Villa Olivetta.
Above: The terraced gardens are filled with romantic walkways and olive, eucalyptus and cypress groves.
Right: The exterior of Stefano Gabbana's Villa Olivetta is in the neo-Medieval style.

Page précédente : Des lits de repos alignés sur la terrasse de la Villa Olivetta de Stefano Gabbana.
En haut : Les jardins en terrasse sont plantés d'oliviers, d'eucalyptus et de cyprès entre lesquels serpentent des allées romantiques.
À droite : La façade néo-médiévale de la Villa Olivetta de Stefano Gabbana.

Vorhergehende Seite: Einladend arrangierte Sonnenliegen auf der Terrasse von Stefano Gabbanas Villa Olivetta.
Oben: Die terrassenförmig angelegten Gärten haben neben vielen romantischen Spazierwegen auch zahlreiche Oliven-, Eukalyptus- und Zypressenhaine aufzuweisen.
Rechts: Von außen präsentiert sich Stefano Gabbanas Villa Olivetta in einem mittelalterlich angehauchten Stil.

New Seaside Interiors   Domenico Dolce & Stefano Gabbana

Right: A view of the landing platform where the designers moor their Riva launch christened "Vergine Maria": it was a Christmas present from Stefano Gabbana to Domenico Dolce.
Below: Guests are treated to spectacular views across the bay of Portofino while they are served lunch.

À droite : Le débarcadère où les stylistes amarrent leur vedette Riva baptisée « Vergine Maria ». Stefano Gabbana l'a offerte à Domenico Dolce en guise de cadeau de Noël.
En bas : Les invités à déjeuner dégustent également les vues spectaculaires sur la baie de Portofino.

Rechts: Blick auf den Anlegeplatz, an dem die Designer ihr auf den Namen „Vergine Maria" (Jungfrau Maria) getauftes Riva-Boot festmachen, übrigens ein Weihnachtsgeschenk von Stefano Gabbana für Domenico Dolce.
Unten: Den Gästen bietet sich eine spektakuläre Aussicht über die Bucht von Portofino, während ihnen der Lunch serviert wird.

Facing page: Black Murano chandeliers and a Lucio Fontana work are reflected in a Louis XV mirror in the drawing room of the Villa Olivetta.
Below: The Doors meets Sino-chic in one of the guestrooms at the Villa Olivetta, with a Chinese-style lantern, red silk brocade and cushions bearing the effigy of Jim Morrison.

Page de droite : Dans le salon de la Villa Olivetta, des lustres de Murano noirs et une œuvre de Lucio Fontana se reflètent dans un miroir Louis XV.
En bas : Dans l'une des chambres d'amis de la Villa Olivetta, les Doors côtoient le chic chinois avec une lanterne en pagode, un brocard de soie rouge et des coussins à l'effigie de Jim Morrison.

Gegenüberliegende Seite: In einem Wohnzimmer der Villa Olivetta spiegeln sich schwarze Kronleuchter aus Murano-Glas und ein Bild von Lucio Fontana in einem Spiegel im Stil Louis XV.
Unten: Im Gästezimmer der Villa Olivetta treffen „The Doors" auf Sino-Schick mit einer Laterne im chinesischem Stil, rotem Seiden-brokat an den Wänden und Kissen mit dem Bildnis von Jim Morrison.

Above: The walls of one corner in the drawing room are covered in an oversized floral print created by artist Michael Lin. Louis XV chairs and a Ferruccio Laviani-designed table stand on a 1960s rug.

En haut : Les murs d'un recoin du salon sont tapissés d'un imprimé de fleurs géantes créé par l'artiste Michael Lin. Sur un tapis des années 60, des chaises Louis XV et une table dessinée par Ferruccio Laviani.

Oben: Die Wände in einer Ecke des Wohnzimmers sind mit einem riesigen Blumendruck überzogen, der von dem Künstler Michael Lin geschaffen wurde. Stühle im Stil Louis XV und ein von Ferruccio Laviani entworfener Tisch stehen auf einem Teppich aus den 1960er-Jahren.

Right: A Virgin with Child hangs to the left of Stefano Gabbana's bed. The mirror and armchairs are examples of the Sicilian Baroque and the bedspread is made from chinchilla.
Below: Ferruccio Laviani created the serpentine sofa, upholstered with ocelot skins, in the Villa Olivetta drawing room. The walls are decorated with fragments of poems by Sarah Casagrande.

À droite : Une Vierge à l'Enfant veille au chevet du lit de Stefano Gabbana recouvert d'un dessus-de-lit en chinchilla près d'un miroir et des fauteuils baroques siciliens.
En bas : Dans le salon de la Villa Olivetta, un canapé sinueux de Ferruccio Laviani tapissé de peaux d'ocelot. Les murs sont ornés de fragments de poèmes de Sarah Casagrande.

Rechts: Eine Jungfrau mit dem Jesuskind hängt links von Stefano Gabbanas Bett. Der Spiegel und die Armsessel sind beispielhaft für den sizilianischen Barock, und der Bettüberwurf wurde aus Chinchillafell gefertigt.
Unten: Das mit Ozelotfellen bezogene Serpentinensofa im Wohnzimmer der Villa Olivetta hat Ferruccio Laviani geschaffen. Die Wände sind mit Fragmenten aus Gedichten von Sarah Casagrande geschmückt.

Above and right: *The kitchen walls and floors at Villa Olivetta have been covered in a mosaic of mirrors and broken pottery from Caltagirone, in Sicily. The lanterns are Venetian.*
Following pages: *One of the guest suites at Villa Olivetta shimmers with thousands of gold mosaic tiles.*

En haut et à droite : *Les murs et le sol de la cuisine de la Villa Olivetta sont recouverts d'une mosaïque en miroirs et fragments de poterie sicilienne provenant de Caltagirone, en Sicile Les lanternes sont vénitiennes.*
Pages suivantes : *Une des suites des invités de la Villa Olivetta scintille de milliers de carreaux de mosaïque dorés.*

Oben und rechts: *Die Küchenwände und -böden in der Villa Olivetta wurden mit einem Mosaik aus Spiegel- und Keramikfliesenscherben überzogen, die aus Caltagirone in Sizilien stammen. Die Lampen sind venezianisch.*
Folgende Seiten: *Tausende von goldenen Glasmosaiksteinchen schimmern in einer der Gästesuiten der Villa Olivetta.*

New Seaside Interiors   Domenico Dolce & Stefano Gabbana

Fiona Swarovski

Capri, Italy

La styliste Fiona Swarovski a visité Capri pour la première fois à dix-huit ans. Après avoir déjeuné près des rochers Faraglioni, elle a remonté la Via Tragara et déclaré : « C'est ici que je veux vivre. » Aujourd'hui, elle crée des accessoires pour de grandes maisons de mode et possède sur l'île une maison bâtie à la fin des années 40 pour la star anglaise du music-hall Gracie Fields. Elle a conservé le sol original en carreaux verts de Vietri, peint les murs couleur corail et ajouté quelques touches éclectiques : des vases en chinoiserie, une collection de verres de Murano, un miroir grotesque et des fauteuils coquillages. À ses yeux, sa terrasse qui jouit d'une vue spectaculaire est « la plus belle du monde. Quand la lune se lève, on dirait une orange. Ensuite, elle devient argentée et trace un chemin de diamants sur la mer. »

Designer Fiona Swarovski was 18 when she visited Capri for the first time. She had lunch near the Faraglioni rocks, walked up the Via Tragara and immediately declared: "This is where I want to live". Today, she creates accessories for luxury fashion brands and owns a house on the island, built in the late 1940s by English music-hall star Gracie Fields. Inside, Swarovski kept the original green Vietri floor tiles and painted the walls coral. She then added various eclectic touches – chinoiserie vases, her collection of Murano glass, a mirror in the "grotesque" style and chairs shaped like shells. For her, the house has "one of the most beautiful terraces in the world". It also has a spectacular view. "When the moon comes up, it looks like an orange," she marvels. "Then, it turns silver and creates a road of diamonds on the sea."

Die Designerin Fiona Swarovski war 18 Jahre, als sie Capri zum ersten Mal besuchte. Kaum hatte sie bei den Faraglioni-Felsen zu Mittag gespeist und war die Via Tragara entlangflaniert, als sie auch schon entschieden erklärte: „Hier möchte ich leben." Heute entwirft sie Accessoires für Modemarken der Luxusklasse und besitzt ein Haus auf der Insel, das Gracie Fields, der englische Music-Hall-Star, in den 1940er-Jahren für sich hatte errichten lassen. Im Inneren behielt Fiona die originalen grünlichen Vietri-Fußbodenfliesen bei, die Wände ließ sie korallenrosa streichen. Hinzu kamen einige eklektische Akzente – Chinoiserie-Vasen, ihre Sammlung von Murano-Glas, ein Spiegel im „grotesken" Stil und muschelförmige Stühle. Für sie hat das Haus „eine der schönsten Terrassen der Welt" und dazu eine atemberaubende Aussicht. „Wenn der Mond aufgeht, gleicht er einer Orange", sagt sie verzaubert, „dann wird er zu Silber und zeichnet eine funkelnde Straße aus Diamanten auf das Wasser."

Tiled Treasure
Positano, Italy

Quand les architectes Claudio Lazzarini et Carl Pickering ont vu pour la première fois cette villa du XVIIIe siècle, elle était « incroyablement délabrée ». En partie effondrée dans les années 20, elle prenait l'eau et n'était plus habitée depuis plus d'un demi-siècle. Pour un couple de quinquagénaires australiens, ils ont aménagé un séjour dans l'orangerie avec ses six mètres sous plafond, inséré des portes en bronze à canon sous les arches néoclassiques et converti la citerne en piscine marocaine. Toutefois, le plus saisissant, ce sont les quatre structures en acier couvertes de 3 000 carreaux anciens de Vietri. Sur les murs, une collection de suzani du XIXe siècle achève le décor. L'idée, selon Pickering, était d'évoquer le glamour des années 60, « quand la côte amalfitaine attirait des célébrités comme Lee Radziwill et Jackie Onasssis ».

When architects Claudio Lazzarini and Carl Pickering first saw this 18th-century villa, it was "incredibly rundown". It had suffered a structural collapse in the 1920s, was letting in water and had been uninhabited since the 1950s. For a 50-something Australian couple, they transformed the former conservatory into a six-metre-high living room, inserted huge gunmetal doors into the Neoclassical arches and created a Moroccan-style pool by enlarging a cistern. The most striking features, however, are four steel-framed elements, covered in some 3,000 antique Vietri tiles. A collection of 19th-century Suzanis on the walls add yet more visual drama. The idea, asserts Pickering, was to create a touch of 1960s glamour. "It's the image of what the Amalfi coast was like then, when visitors included people like Lee Radziwill and Jackie Onassis."

Als die Architekten Claudio Lazzarini und Carl Pickering zum ersten Mal diese Villa aus dem 18. Jahrhundert sahen, war sie „unglaublich heruntergekommen". In den 1920er-Jahren waren tragende Teile eingestürzt, sodass der Bau nicht mehr wassergeschützt war. Seit den 1950er-Jahren war das Haus zudem unbewohnt. Für ein australisches Ehepaar in den Fünfzigern verwandelten sie den ehemaligen Wintergarten in einen Wohnraum mit sechs Meter hoher Decke, setzten riesige Metalltüren in die klassizistischen Bögen und erweiterten eine Zisterne zu einem Pool im marokkanischen Stil. Der faszinierendste Blickfang aber sind die vier Konstruktionen aus stahlgerahmten Elementen, die mit über 3000 antiken Vietri-Fliesen gekachelt sind. Eine Sammlung von Suzanis aus dem 19. Jahrhundert an den Wänden setzt zusätzliche dramatische Akzente. Laut Pickering galt es, die 1960er-Jahre anklingen zu lassen und „den Glamour der Küste von Amalfi wieder heraufzubeschwören, als Lee Radziwill und Jackie Onassis zu ihren Besuchern zählten."

Below and facing page: A ribbon of vintage 18th- and 19th-century Vietri tiles winds its way across the main living room.
Following pages: As the ribbon descends, it is transformed into the dining table. On either side stand Eero Saarinen's "Tulip" chairs. The kitchen units are from Boffi and the design of the brushed-steel spots was inspired by those fitted in the original 1970s Concorde.

En bas et page de droite : Un ruban de carreaux de Vietri du XVIIIᵉ et XIXᵉ siècle s'insinue dans le salon principal.
Pages suivantes : En chemin, le ruban devient table de salle à manger. De part et d'autre, des chaises « Tulip » d'Eero Saarinen. Les éléments de cuisine viennent de chez Boffi et les spots en acier brossé s'inspirent de ceux du premier Concorde des années 70.

Unten und gegenüberliegende Seite: Ein Band aus erlesenen Vietri-Fliesen aus dem 18. und 19. Jahrhundert zieht sich über die Wände bis in den zentralen Wohnraum.
Folgende Seiten: Das von oben nach unten verlaufende Band verwandelt sich in den von Eero Saarinens „Tulip"-Stühlen flankierten Esstisch. Die Kücheneinrichtung stammt von Boffi, und das Design der Spotlights aus poliertem Edelstahl orientiert sich an den Leuchtkörpern der ersten Concorde aus den 1970er-Jahren.

Previous pages: On the terrace overlooking the Gulf of Salerno, a former cistern has been transformed into a Moroccan-style pool. Cushions are arranged on a platform covered with brand-new Vietri tiles.
Above and facing page: Hefty gunmetal doors have been fitted with bullet-proof glass and inserted into Neoclassical arches.

Pages précédentes : Sur la terrasse qui domine le golfe de Salerne, l'ancienne citerne a été transformée en piscine de style marocain. Les coussins sont disposés sur une plateforme tapissée de carreaux de Vietri modernes.
En haute et page droite : Des portes massives en bronze à canon ont été équipées de vitres pare-balles et insérées sous les arches néoclassiques.

Vorhergehende Seiten: Auf der Terrasse mit Blick auf den Golf von Salerno wurde eine ehemalige Zisterne in einen Pool im marokkanischen Stil verwandelt. Kissen sind dekorativ auf einer Plattform mit modernen Vietri-Fliesen verteilt.
Oben und gegenüberliegende Seite: Hohe Metalltüren wurden mit kugelsicherem Glas versehen und in klassizistische Bögen eingepasst.

Above: Stairs lead up to a master bedroom and the "Flying Sofa" seating area, which is cantilevered two metres into the main space. Antonio Citterio's "Apta" chair is slip-covered in raw linen.
Right: The red sofa is a modular system designed by Francesco Binfaré for Edra.

En haut : Des marches mènent à la chambre des maîtres et au « canapé volant », un coin salon qui s'avance de deux mètres au-dessus de l'espace principal. Le fauteuil « Apta » d'Antonio Citterio est tapissé d'une housse en lin brut.
À droite : Le sofa modulaire rouge a été conçu par Francesco Binfaré pour Edra.

Oben: Eine kleine Treppe führt zu einem Schlafzimmer und zu dem „Flying Sofa" genannten Sitzbereich, der frei schwebend zwei Meter weit in den Hauptraum vorkragt. Antonio Citterios „Apta"-Stuhl hat eine Stoffhusse aus grobem, naturbelassenem Leinen.
Rechts: Das rote Sofa ist ein von Francesco Binfaré für Edra entworfenes modulares System.

Right: An Antonio Citterio-designed bed stands on another steel-framed platform covered with vintage Vietri tiles. The bedspread is made from a Manuel Canovas striped chenille.
Below: In the "Flying Sofa" seating area is one of the six 19th-century Suzanis, which add a dramatic touch to the décor.

À droite : Un lit dessiné par Antonio Citterio est posé sur une autre plateforme tapissée d'anciens carreaux de Vietri. Le dessus-de-lit est en chenille rayée de chez Manuel Canovas.
En bas : Dans le coin salon baptisé « le canapé volant », un des six suzani du XIXe siècle ajoute une belle touche de couleur au décor.

Rechts: Ein Antonio-Citterio-Bett auf einer weiteren stahlgerahmten, mit alten Vietri-Fliesen gekachelten Plattform. Der Bettüberwurf besteht aus einem gestreiften Chenillestoff von Manuel Canovas.
Unten: Der „Flying Sofa" genannte Sitzbereich zeigt einen der sechs Suzanis aus dem 19. Jahrhundert, die dem Dekor einen dramatischen Effekt geben.

Domenico Dolce & Stefano Gabbana

Stromboli, Italy

Pour Domenico Dolce et Stefano Gabbana, Stromboli fut un coup de foudre. « L'île est magique. On y a toujours voulu une maison », confie Stefano Gabbana. Au point qu'ils ont acheté la première qu'ils ont visitée, deux bâtiments blanchis à la chaux reliés par une série de patios et de terrasses. Le volcan le plus actif d'Europe gronde juste au-dessus. « Son énergie et son mystère nous fascinent. » À leurs pieds s'étire une plage de sable noir où, l'été, Naomi Campbell et de nombreuses célébrités amies les rejoignent pour faire la fête. L'intérieur est une débauche d'antiquités, d'imprimés animaliers et de tons vifs. « L'île est tellement noir et blanc, nous avons voulu un décor étincelant et coloré », explique Stefano Gabbana. C'est leur retraite idéale au mois d'août. « C'est calme, sans paparazzi ; on s'y sent libres et heureux. »

© Stefano Guindani

Domenico Dolce and Stefano Gabbana fell in love with Stromboli the first time they saw it. "It's a magical island," enthuses Stefano Gabbana. "We have always known we wanted to have a house there." They actually bought the first place they visited – a compound of two whitewashed houses, linked by a series of patios and terraces. Above it growls Europe's most active volcano: "It fascinates us because of its energy and the mystery it exudes," asserts the design duo. Down on the shore is a black sand beach where Naomi Campbell and many other celebrity friends have partied with them during their summer holidays. The interiors have been decorated with a riot of antiques and animal prints, as well as tons of bright hues. "The island is so black-and-white, therefore we wanted the interiors to be shiny and colourful," states Stefano Gabbana. For both of them, it provides the perfect escape in August. As they say: "It's calm, there are no paparazzi and we feel free and happy."

Für Domenico Dolce und Stefano Gabbana war Stromboli Liebe auf den ersten Blick. „Es ist eine magische Insel", schwärmt Stefano Gabbana. „Wir wussten schon immer, dass wir dort ein Haus haben wollten." Tatsächlich erwarben sie schon die erste Immobilie, die sie besichtigten – ein Grundstück mit zwei durch Patios und Terrassen verbundenen weiß getünchten Häusern. Über ihnen grollt der aktivste Vulkan Europas. „Er fasziniert uns wegen seiner Energie, seiner geheimnisvollen Ausstrahlung", erklärt das Designer-Duo. Unten am Meer erstreckt sich ein schwarzer Sandstrand, wo schon Naomi Campbell und viele andere Berühmtheiten in ihren Sommerferien mit ihnen Feste feierten. Die Interieurs wurden mit einer Fülle von Antiquitäten sowie verschiedenen Tiermustern dekoriert und in strahlend bunte Farbtöne getaucht. „Die Insel ist so schwarz-weiß, daher wünschten wir farbenfrohe und strahlende Innenräume", erklärt Stefano Gabbana. Für beide ist das Haus das perfekte Fluchtziel im August, denn: „Es ist ruhig, es gibt keine Paparazzi, und wir fühlen uns frei und glücklich."

Previous page: The blues of the sea and sky are echoed in the table in front of the house.
Right: Three "Outdoor Sun Lounge Chairs" from Alias are lined up on one of the numerous terraces.
Below: The house lies in the shadow of Europe's most active volcano, which blows up sparks and flaming rock every 20 minutes.

Page précédente : Les bleus de la mer et du ciel se retrouvent dans la table devant la maison.
À droite : Trois « Outdoor Sun Lounge Chairs » d'Alias alignées sur l'une des nombreuses terrasses.
En bas : La maison est nichée au pied du volcan le plus actif d'Europe. Il crache des étincelles et des roches incandescentes toutes les 20 minutes.

Vorhergehende Seite: Das Blau von Meer und Himmel scheint sich in der Tischplatte vor dem Haus zu spiegeln.
Rechts: Drei „Outdoor Sun Lounge Chairs" von Alias sind auf einer der zahlreichen Terrassen aufgereiht.
Unten: Das Haus liegt im Schatten des aktivsten europäischen Vulkans, der alle 20 Minuten Funken und glühendes Gestein ausspuckt.

Above: For Stefano Gabbana, the house's terraces are "the symbol of the communion between the house and the nature around it". This one is situated off the dining room at the back.

Right: Dolce and Gabbana's 12-bedroom property actually consists of two traditional houses linked by a series of terraces and patios. They opted to keep the exteriors as they were.

En haut : Pour Stefano Gabbana, les nombreuses terrasses sont « le symbole de la communion entre la maison et son environnement ». Celle-ci se situe à l'arrière de la maison et communique avec la salle à manger.

À droite : La propriété, qui compte 12 chambres, est en fait constituée de deux maisons traditionnelles reliées par une série de terrasses et de patios. Dolce et Gabbana ont choisi de conserver les extérieurs tels quels.

Oben: Für Stefano Gabbana sind die Terrassen „ein Symbol der Verbindung zwischen dem Haus und allem, was es umgibt." Die hier gezeigte liegt neben dem Esszimmer auf der Rückseite.

Rechts: Dolces und Gabbanas Anwesen mit zwölf Schlafzimmern besteht aus zwei traditionellen Häusern, die untereinander durch zahlreiche Terrassen und Patios verbunden sind. Die beiden beschlossen, die Außenanlagen in ihrem ursprünglichen Zustand zu belassen.

Above: Stefano Gabbana refers to their decorating style as "tasty kitsch". Here, images of movie stars, popular religious paintings and handmade lace curtains adorn the dining-room terrace.
Right: Folkloric Sicilian ceramic heads are used as candleholders.
Facing page: With the addition of carpets and cushions, the large terrace is transformed into an outdoor living room.

En haut : Stefano Gabbana qualifie leur style de décoration de « kitsch savoureux ». La terrasse de la salle à manger est ornée de photos de stars de cinéma, de peintures religieuses populaires et de rideaux en dentelle artisanaux.
À droite : Des têtes en céramiques siciliennes converties en bougeoirs.
Page de droite : À l'aide de tapis et de coussins, la grande terrasse a été transformée en séjour extérieur.

Oben: Stefano Gabbana nennt den hier angewandten Dekorationsstil „Tasty Kitsch". Porträts von Filmstars, volkstümliche religiöse Gemälde und handgearbeitete Spitzenvorhänge schmücken die Terrasse mit Essplatz.
Rechts: Folkloristische sizilianische Keramikköpfe dienen als Kerzenhalter.
Gegenüberliegende Seite: Durch die Ausstattung mit vielen Teppichen und Kissen wird die große Terrasse zu einem Wohnzimmer im Freien.

Right: The bright pink room is where Naomi Campbell sleeps when she is a house guest. The 17th-century Sicilian chair in the foreground has been re-upholstered in a Dolce & Gabbana velvet tiger print.
Below: Two sitting rooms are separated by patchwork curtains, made from velvets, silks and satins collected by the designers during their travels.

À droite : La chambre rose vif est celle où dort Naomi Campbell quand elle est de passage. Le fauteuil sicilien du XVIIᵉ siècle au premier plan a été retapissé avec un imprimé tigre en velours de Dolce & Gabbana.
En bas : Deux petits salons sont séparés par des rideaux en patchwork fabriqués avec des morceaux de satin, de velours et de soie glanés par les deux stylistes au cours de leurs voyages.

Rechts: In diesem Zimmer in kräftigem Pink schläft Naomi Campbell, wenn sie zu Gast ist. Der sizilianische Stuhl aus dem 17. Jahrhundert im Vordergrund wurde mit einem Samtstoff von Dolce & Gabbana im Tigerdruck neu bezogen.
Unten: Zwei Wohnzimmer werden durch Patchwork-Vorhänge getrennt; sie entstanden aus von den Designern auf ihren Reisen gesammelten Samt-, Seiden- und Satinstoffen.

Above: In the "Leopard" bedroom are two tongue-in-cheek icons depicting "Santo Stefano" and "Santo Domenico". They are the work of Andrea Martini, a friend of the designers.
Right: Cobalt blue is only one of the vivid colours used inside the house. In the far corner stand a Baroque procession staff and a rustic farm chair found at an antique market in Palermo.
Following pages: The dining room and kitchen are clad in a crazy mosaic of vintage tiles from Caltagirone in Sicily. The coloured chandeliers were designed by Domenico Dolce himself.

En haut : La chambre « léopard » avec ses icônes humoristiques re-présentant « Santo Stefano » et « Santo Domenico ». Elles ont été peintes par Andrea Martini, un ami des stylistes.
À droite : Le bleu cobalt est l'une des couleurs vives utilisées dans la maison. Au fond, un bâton de procession baroque et une chaise de ferme rustique trouvée sur une foire d'antiquaires à Palerme.
Pages suivantes : La cuisine et la salle à manger sont tapissées d'une mosaïque délirante réalisée avec d'anciens carreaux de céramique provenant de la manufacture sicilienne de Caltagirone. Les lustres ont été créés par Domenico Dolce.

Oben: Im „Leopard"-Schlafzimmer hängen zwei ironisch gemeinte Heiligenbilder: „Santo Stefano" und „Santo Domenico". Sie sind das Werk von Andrea Martini, einem Freund der Designer.
Rechts: Kobaltblau ist nur eine der im Haus verwendeten Farben. Hinten in der Ecke stehen ein barocker Prozessionsstab und ein auf einem Antiquitätenmarkt in Palermo gefundener schlichter Bauern-stuhl.
Folgende Seiten: Das Esszimmer und die Küche wurden mit einem wilden Mosaik aus antiken Kacheln, die aus Caltagirone in Sizilien stammen, verkleidet. Die bunten Kronleuchter sind Entwürfe von Domenico Dolce aus venezianischem und böhmischem Glas.

Belquis Zahir
Filicudi, Italy

The Aeolian island of Filicudi reminds designer and decorator Belquis Zahir of her native Afghanistan. "It has the simplicity of a place lost in time," she affirms. Her own house is certainly redolent of that. It is situated in Contrada Canale, a village of 12 houses with only three off-season inhabitants. When she found it, the structure had lost its roof. She rebuilt that, covered all the walls in limestone and created internal connections between the different rooms (before, you had to step outside to go from one to another). The original oven was transformed into a shower and just a few Oriental touches added. Among them, the traditional Afghan *chor poi* bed on the terrace. Currently, Zahir is working on the renovation of a second house, located in an abandoned village accessed by donkey path. "It's even more back-to-nature... if that's possible."

Previous page: An Afghan "chor poi" bed made from wood and vegetable rope stands on a terrace overlooking the Mediterranean. The two small ottomans are from Ikea.
Above and right: Zahir has breakfast and dinner on this terrace in front of the house. She rebuilt the roof in typical Eolian style, using canes and wooden beams. The limestone was acquired from Fratelli Spadaro in Rosolini (Sicily). The niches on the façade were originally intended for oil lamps.

Page précédente : Sur la terrasse qui surplombe la Méditerranée, un lit chor poi afghan en bois et corde végétale. Les deux petits poufs viennent de chez Ikea.
En haut et à droite : Zahir prend ses petits déjeuners et dîne sur cette terrasse devant la maison. Elle a reconstruit le toit dans le style des maisons des îles Éoliennes, avec des joncs et des poutres en bois. La chaux provient de chez les Fratelli Spadaro à Rosolini (Sicile). Les niches de la façade servaient autrefois à accueillir des lampes à huile.

Vorhergehende Seite: Eine afghanische Chor-poi-Liege aus Holz und geflochtenen Pflanzenschnüren auf einer Terrasse mit Blick aufs Mittelmeer. Die beiden runden Sitzkissen stammen von Ikea.
Oben und rechts: Zahir pflegt auf dieser Terrasse vor dem Haus zu frühstücken und zu Abend zu essen. Das Schatten spendende Vordach ließ sie aus Holzbalken und Rohrgeflecht im typischen äolischen Stil anfertigen. Der Kalkstein wurde bei der Firma Fratelli Spadaro in Rosolini (Sizilien) erworben. Die Nischen in der Fassade waren ursprünglich für Öllampen gedacht.

Right: *The guest bedroom on the lower level. The sculpture chair was made by an artist called Antonio, who used to live on Filicudi.*
Below: *The terrace in front of the master bedroom. Habitat candle-holders stand on a table, which used to belong to a glass factory in Rome.*

À droite : *La chambre d'amis au niveau inférieur. La chaise sculpture est l'œuvre d'Antonio, un artiste qui vivait autrefois à Filicudi.*
En bas : *La terrasse devant la chambre principale. Des bougeoirs de chez Habitat sont posés sur une table provenant d'une ancienne ver-rerie de Rome.*

Rechts: *Das Gästezimmer im unteren Geschoss. Der wie eine Skulp-tur wirkende Stuhl ist das Werk eines Künstlers namens Antonio, der auf der Insel lebte.*
Unten: *Die Terrasse vor dem Schlafzimmer. Kerzenhalter von Habitat stehen auf einem Tisch, der aus einer Glasfabrik in Rom stammt.*

Above: A view from the living room into the master bedroom. Zahir designed both the fireplace and the sofa. The latter is upholstered in an Indian cotton.
Right and facing page: The old bread oven was turned into a shower. A mirror bought at an antique market in Palermo hangs above an old baptismal font.

En haut : Vue du séjour avec, au le fond, la chambre principale. Zahir a dessiné la cheminée et le canapé. Ce dernier est tapissé d'une cotonnade indienne.
À droite et page de droite : L'ancien four à pain a été reconverti en douche. Un miroir déniché sur un marché d'antiquaires à Palerme est accroché au-dessus d'un lavabo qui servait autrefois de fonts baptismaux.

Oben: Blick aus dem Wohnzimmer ins Schlafzimmer. Sowohl der Kamin als auch das mit indischem Baumwollstoff bezogene Sofa sind Entwürfe Zahirs.
Rechts und gegenüberliegende Seite: Der alte Backofen wurde zur Duschkabine. Ein Spiegel, Zufallsfund auf einem Antiquitätenmarkt in Palermo, hängt über einem ehemaligen Taufbecken.

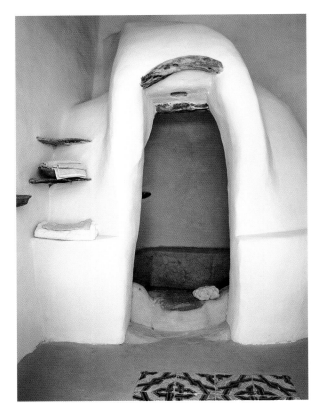

Paul Barthelemy

Alicudi, Italy

Pour l'architecte Paul Barthelemy, l'absence de voitures, de routes et de développement fait tout le charme d'Alicudi. « C'est très sauvage », explique-t-il, « les maisons ont conservé l'esprit de leurs premiers occupants, des agriculteurs. » C'est le cas de la sienne, très primitive, perchée à 100 m au-dessus de la mer à l'est de l'île. Sans doute construite au XIXe siècle, elle compte trois chambres, une cuisine et une salle de bains. Il n'y a pas d'électricité à l'extérieur et la terrasse est illuminée le soir avec des bougies et des lampes à huile. La mezzanine dans l'une des chambres servait probablement autrefois à entreposer le foin. L'accès à l'île est tout aussi rudimentaire : il n'y a pas de port, uniquement une jetée. « Par mauvais temps, il n'est pas rare d'être coupé du monde. »

For architect Paul Barthelemy, the charm of the Aeolian island Alicudi is that there are no cars, no roads and little development. "It's still wild," he says, "and the houses have retained the spirit of their original inhabitants: farmers." That's certainly the case with his own house, perched some 100 metres above the sea on the east of the island. He believes that it probably dates back to the 19th century. It consists of three bedrooms, a kitchen and a bathroom, and remains quite primitive. There is no electricity on the outside of the house. Instead, candles and oil lamps provide light on the terrace. Inside, a mezzanine in one of the bedrooms was no doubt previously used to store hay. The means of getting on and off Alicudi are equally rudimentary. There is no port... only a jetty. "In bad weather," he says, "there's a risk you could be stranded."

Für den Architekten Paul Barthelemy liegt der Charme der Äolischen Insel Alicudi in der Tatsache, dass es dort weder Autos noch Straßen und kaum kommerzielle Entwicklungen gibt. „Es ist hier immer noch recht urwüchsig", sagt er, „und die Häuser haben den Geist ihrer ursprünglichen bäuerlichen Bewohner beibehalten." Das trifft ohne jeden Zweifel für sein eigenes Haus zu, das im Osten der Insel etwa 100 Meter über dem Meer liegt. Seiner Meinung nach stammt es aus dem 19. Jahrhundert. Es besteht aus drei Schlafzimmern, Küche und Bad und hat sich eine gewisse primitive Schlichtheit bewahrt. Außen am Haus gibt es keinen elektrischen Anschluss; nur Kerzen und Öllampen beleuchten die Terrasse. Im Inneren verweist ein Zwischenstock in einem der Schlafzimmer auf seine einstige Rolle als Heuspeicher. Auch die An- und Abfahrtswege sind rudimentär. Es gibt keinen Hafen, nur eine Anlegestelle. „Bei schlechtem Wetter", sagt Paul, „besteht das Risiko, dass man festsitzt."

Previous pages: Barthelemy rebuilt the pergola on the terrace. The green table comes from his family home on Sicily and the wooden chairs were bought with the house.
Facing page: Oil lamps are used to light the exterior of the house.
Above: The mezzanine in one of the bedrooms was probably once used to store hay. The beds are made from wrought iron.
Right: The tiles in the kitchen are believed to date from the 19th century.

Pages précédentes : Barthelemy a reconstruit la pergola sur la terrasse. La table verte vient de sa demeure familiale en Sicile et les chaises en bois se trouvaient déjà dans la maison.
Page de gauche : L'extérieur de la maison est éclairé avec des lampes à huile.
En haut : La mezzanine dans l'une des chambres servait probablement autrefois à entreposer le foin. Les lits sont en fer forgé.
À droite : Le carrelage de la cuisine daterait du XIXᵉ siècle.

Vorhergehende Seiten: Barthelemy baute die Pergola auf der Terrasse wieder auf. Der grüne Tisch stammt aus seinem Elternhaus in Sizilien, und die Holzstühle wurden zusammen mit dem Haus erworben.
Gegenüberliegende Seite: Petroleumlampen dienen als Außenbeleuchtung.
Oben: Der Zwischenstock in einem der Schlafzimmer diente einst wohl als Heuspeicher. Die Betten wurden aus Schmiedeeisen gefertigt.
Rechts: Die Kacheln in der Küche stammen wahrscheinlich aus dem 19. Jahrhundert.

José Gandía-Blasco

Ibiza, Spain

José Gandía-Blasco dirige une société familiale de décoration. À l'origine, elle ne produisait que des textiles, jusqu'à ce qu'il se mette en quête de meubles d'extérieur pour sa maison à Ibiza. « Tout était tellement traditionnel ! On ne trouvait rien de simple et de contemporain. » Il a donc décidé de créer sa propre ligne avec son architecte, Ramón Esteve. La maison en question est située près de Na Xemena, un hameau isolé au nord de l'île. De l'extérieur, on dirait une série de fincas traditionnelles modernisées par l'ouverture de grandes fenêtres. L'intérieur est délibérément austère, dépouillé et blanc. « La maison s'harmonise avec l'esprit des lieux, qui est très paisible », affirme-t-il. « C'est comme un monastère perdu dans les falaises. »

José Gandía-Blasco runs a homeware company founded by his family. It used to produce just textiles. Then, he began looking for outdoor furniture for his own house on Ibiza. "Everything was very traditional," he recalls. "We couldn't find anything as contemporary and simple as we wanted." So, he decided to develop his own collection with his architect, Ramón Esteve. The house in question is situated near the remote hamlet of Na Xemena on the island's north coast. From the outside, it looks like a series of traditional fincas, given a modern twist by the insertion of large windows. Inside, it is deliberately austere. The walls are white and the furnishings quite sparse. Still, that's just how he likes it. "The spirit of the area is very peaceful and the house fits in well with that," he insists. "It's like a monastery lost on the cliffs."

José Gandía-Blasco leitet eine von seiner Familie gegründete Homewear-Firma, die ursprünglich ganz auf Textilien spezialisiert war. Eines Tages aber begann er, sich nach Terrassen- und Gartenmöbeln für sein Haus in Ibiza umzuschauen. „Alles war sehr traditionell", erinnert er sich. „Wir konnten nichts finden, das so zeitgemäß und schlicht war, wie wir wollten." Daher beschloss er, zusammen mit seinem Architekten Ramón Esteve eine eigene Kollektion zu entwickeln. Das besagte Haus liegt in der Nähe des abgelegenen Dorfes Na Xemena an der Nordküste der Insel. Von außen sieht es wie eine Reihe von traditionellen Fincas aus, die durch eingesetzte große Fenster eine moderne Note erhalten haben. Das Interieur ist bewusst schlicht gehalten. Die Wände erstrahlen in reinem Weiß, und die Möblierung ist recht streng. Doch gerade so gefällt es ihm. „Der Geist der Landschaft ist sehr friedlich, und das Haus passt sehr gut hinein", betont er. „Es ist wie ein einsames Kloster auf den Klippen."

Below: *Two sculptures from Indonesia stand at the foot of the stairs.*
Facing page: *A sunken concrete tub sits in the corner of one of the bedrooms. The taps are from Roca and the standing light is the "Dorica" model, designed by Jordi Miralbell and Mariona Raventós.*

En bas : *Au pied des escaliers, deux sculptures indonésiennes.*
Page de droite : *Dans un coin d'une des chambres, une baignoire encastrée en béton. La robinetterie vient de chez Rocca. Le lampadaire « Dorica » a été dessiné par Jordi Miralbell et Mariona Raventós.*

Unten: *Zwei Skulpturen aus Indonesien am Fuß der Treppe.*
Gegenüberliegende Seite: *Eines der Schlafzimmer besitzt eine im Boden versenkte Wanne aus Beton. Die Wasserhähne sind von Roca, und die Stehlampe ist das von Jordi Miralbell und Mariona Raventós entworfene Modell „Dorica".*

Previous pages: *The construction of the house inspired owner José Gandía-Blasco and architect Ramón Esteve to design a collection of outdoor furniture made from anodized aluminium. On the terrace are their "Chill" daybeds, and a table and chairs from the "Na Xemena" line.*
Above: *The iroko dining table and chairs were also designed by Gandía-Blasco and Esteve. The pendant lights are from Santa & Cole.*

Pages précédentes : *La construction de la maison a inspiré à son propriétaire José Gandía-Blasco et à son architecte Ramón Esteve une ligne de meubles d'extérieur en aluminium anodisé. Sur la terrasse, leurs lits de repos « Chill » ainsi qu'une table et des chaises de leur collection « Na Xemena ».*
En haute : *La table de salle à manger et les chaises en iroko ont également été dessinées par Gandía-Blasco et Esteve. Les luminaires viennent de chez Santa & Cole.*

Vorhergehende Seiten: *Der Bau des Hauses inspirierte den Bauherrn José Gandía-Blasco und seinen Architekten Ramón Esteve dazu, eine Kollektion von Gartenmöbeln aus eloxiertem Aluminium zu entwerfen. Auf der Terrasse sind ihre „Chill"-Liegen sowie ein Tisch und Stühle aus der „Na Xemena"-Linie zu sehen.*
Oben: *Ebenfalls Entwürfe von Gandía-Blasco und Esteve sind der Esstisch aus Irokoholz mit Stühlen. Die Hängelampen stammen von Santa & Cole.*

New Seaside Interiors   José Gandía-Blasco

Jacques Grange
Carvalhal, Portugal

Pendant l'année, le décorateur Jacques Grange mène grand train. Habitant à Paris dans l'ancien appartement de Colette au Palais Royal, ses clients incluent Caroline de Monaco et Yves Saint Laurent. Mais quand vient le mois d'août, son compagnon l'antiquaire Pierre Passebon et lui s'échappent dans leur retraite d'une étonnante simplicité dans la région d'Alentejo. Cachée derrière des dunes, on y accède par une piste en terre. Elle est composée de trois cabanes abritant la cuisine/salle à manger, une chambre d'amis et la suite des maîtres. Le séjour est situé dans une vieille étable. Le décor est volontairement sobre, avec quelques touches portugaises, des textiles africains et plusieurs meubles signés. « J'ai toujours rêvé d'une maison sur une plage intacte et tranquille », explique Grange. « Pour moi, c'est un peu le paradis sur terre. »

For most of the year, decorator Jacques Grange's life is full of sophistication. He lives in writer Colette's former flat in Paris's Palais Royal and has a client list that includes Caroline of Monaco and Yves Saint Laurent. In August, however, he and his antique dealer partner Pierre Passebon escape to a beach house in the Alentejo region, which is striking in its simplicity. Tucked behind lofty dunes, it consists of four huts, accessed via a dirt road. One houses the kitchen and dining room, another a guestroom and a third the master suite. The living room, meanwhile, is located in an old animal barn. The interiors are deliberately simple. There are local Portuguese touches, African fabrics and a handful of signed pieces. "My dream was always to have a house on a quiet, untouched beach," explains Grange. "For me, it's a kind of paradise on Earth."

Der Innenarchitekt Jacques Grange bewegt sich die meiste Zeit des Jahres in einem äußerst eleganten Ambiente. Er bewohnt das ehemalige Apartment der Schriftstellerin Colette im Pariser Palais Royal, und in seiner Kundenkartei finden sich Namen wie Caroline von Monaco und Yves Saint Laurent. Doch im August fliehen er und sein Partner, der Antiquitätenhändler Pierre Passebon, in ein erstaunlich einfaches Strandhaus in die portugiesische Region Alentejo. Es besteht aus vier Hütten hinter hohen Dünen, zu denen ein Sandweg führt. Eine Hütte enthält die Küche und das Esszimmer, die andere das Gästezimmer und eine dritte das Schlafzimmer. Das Wohnzimmer ist in einem alten Stall untergebracht. Die Inneneinrichtung wurde bewusst schlicht gehalten. Sie zeigt portugiesische Akzente, afrikanische Stoffe und eine Handvoll signierter Objekte. „Mein Traum war es stets, ein Haus an einem ruhigen, unberührten Strand zu besitzen", erklärt Grange. „Für mich ist dies das Paradies auf Erden."

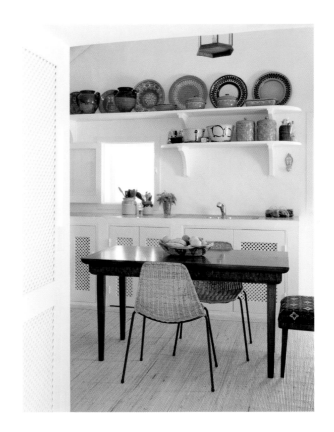

Previous pages: Jacques Grange (right) with his partner Pierre Passebon. A Syrian "kilim" and a 1960s wicker chair in front of the former animal barn, now home to the living room.
Right: Jean Royère chairs and a table designed by Carlo Pessina in the kitchen. The ceramics are Portuguese.
Below: In front of the hut housing the guest quarters is a bench covered in a cotton fabric from Sardinia. The rug is from the south of India and the blue plant pots by Edouard Cazaux.

Pages précédentes : Jacques Grange (à droite) avec son compagnon Pierre Passebon. Devant l'ancienne étable, qui accueille aujourd'hui le séjour, un kilim syrien et une chaise en osier des années 60.
À droite : Dans la cuisine, des chaises de Jean Royère autour d'une table de Carlo Pessina. Les céramiques sont portugaises.
En bas : Devant la cabane des invités, un banc tapissé d'une cotonnade sarde. Le tapis vient du sud de l'Inde et les pots de fleurs bleus sont d'Édouard Cazaux.

Vorhergehende Seiten: Jacques Grange (rechts) mit seinem Partner Pierre Passebon. Ein syrischer Kelim und ein Korbsessel aus den 1960er-Jahren vor dem einstigen Stall, jetzt Wohnzimmer.
Rechts: Jean-Royère-Stühle und ein von Carlo Pessina entworfener Tisch in der Küche. Die Keramiken sind portugiesischer Herkunft.
Unten: Vor der Hütte für Gäste steht eine mit Baumwollstoff aus Sardinien bezogene Bank. Der Teppich stammt aus Südindien, und die blauen Töpfe sind von Edouard Cazaux.

Above: *The teak table and benches at the end of the living room are from Bali. There are also cushions made from African fabrics, a straw and leather rug from Morocco and a curvaceous coffee table from Amazonia.*
Right: *At the other end of the living room, a buffalo's head surveys a Roger Capron coffee table and a copy of a 1930s sofa in rope by Audoux-Minet.*

En haut : *La table et les bancs en teck au fond du séjour viennent de Bali. Les coussins du canapé sont en tissus africains, le tapis en paille et cuir vient du Maroc, la petite table basse aux formes arrondies d'Amazonie.*
À droite : *À l'autre extrémité du séjour, un crâne de buffle domine une table basse de Roger Capron et la copie d'un canapé en corde des années 30 d'Audoux-Minet.*

Oben: *Der Tisch und die Bänke aus Teakholz im hinteren Teil des Wohnzimmers kommen aus Bali. Dazu Kissen aus afrikanischen Stoffen, ein Stroh-und-Leder-Teppich aus Marokko und ein geschweiftes Tischchen aus dem Amazonasgebiet.*
Rechts: *Am anderen Ende des Wohnzimmers blickt der Schädel eines Büffels auf einen Sofatisch von Roger Capron und den Nachbau eines Flechtsofas aus den 1930er-Jahren von Audoux-Minet.*

Below: Grange adapted a "Less is More" approach for the master bathroom.

En bas : Dans la salle de bains, Grange a adopté une démarche minimaliste.

Unten: Beim Badezimmer hat sich Grange für das Prinzip „weniger ist mehr" entschieden.

Facing page: A panel of ceramic tiles created by Jean Mayodon in the 1930s hangs above the rustic master bed. The two lamps are early 20th-century French.
Above: In one corner of the master bedroom, collages by Yves Saint Laurent sit on a 19th-century "cartonnier". The chair comes from the Villa Taylor, a famous Art Deco residence in Marrakech.

Page de gauche : Au-dessus du grand lit rustique, un panneau en carreaux de céramique créé par Jean Mayodon dans les années 30. Les deux lampes françaises datent du début du XXᵉ siècle.
En haut : Dans un coin de la chambre des maîtres, des collages d'Yves Saint Laurent sur un cartonnier du XIXᵉ siècle. Le fauteuil provient de la Villa Taylor, une célèbre résidence Art Déco de Marrakech.

Gegenüberliegende Seite: Eine Platte aus Keramikkacheln, von Jean Mayodon in den 1930er-Jahren geschaffen, hängt über dem rustikalen Bett. Die beiden französischen Lampen sind frühes 20. Jahrhundert.
Oben: In einer Ecke des Schlafzimmers stehen Collagen von Yves Saint Laurent auf einer Kommode aus dem 19. Jahrhundert. Der Stuhl entstammt der Villa Taylor, einer berühmten Art-Deco-Residenz in Marrakesch.

Christina von Rosen

Algarve, Portugal

Quand l'artiste Christina von Rosen est arrivée au Portugal en 1975, elle a exposé ses œuvres et s'est acheté une maison avec les profits. « À l'époque, ça ne coûtait pas cher », se souvient-elle. Ce n'était qu'une petite cabane de pêcheur en pierre de 30 mètres carrés située dans la réserve naturelle de Ria Formosa. Un marais et des dunes la séparent de la mer. Les ruines romaines de Balsa se trouvent à deux pas. Von Rosen a agrandi le rez-de-chaussée et créé des chambres d'amis surmontées de deux terrasses. Quant au décor, c'est une œuvre en évolution perpétuelle. Un soir, alors qu'elle peignait un poisson sur un buffet, « ma main a glissé et il s'est retrouvé avec une cigarette au bec ! ». Accidents artistiques mis à part, son seul souci est le réchauffement de la planète. « À marée haute, il ne reste plus que quelques centimètres entre la mer et le seuil de ma porte. »

When artist Christina von Rosen moved to Portugal in 1975, she held an exhibition of her work and bought a small place with the proceeds. "Houses weren't expensive back then," she recalls. Initially, her current dwelling was equally modest – a tiny, stone fisherman's house of around 30 square metres. Situated in the Ria Formosa nature reserve, it looks out over marshland and dunes towards the sea. Nearby is the former Roman site of Balsa. Von Rosen extended the ground floor and created guest quarters and two terraces above it. As for the décor, she says that it's an ongoing process. One evening, she painted a fish motif onto a cupboard. "My hand slipped and suddenly, one of the fish had a cigarette in its mouth!" Artistic accidents aside, her only worry is global warming. "At high tide, there aren't many centimetres to spare between the sea and the doorstep!"

Als die Künstlerin Christina von Rosen 1975 nach Portugal ging, veranstaltete sie dort eine Ausstellung ihrer Werke und kaufte mit dem Erlös ein kleines Haus. „Damals waren die Häuser hier sehr preiswert", erinnert sie sich. Anfänglich war ihr gegenwärtiges Heim ebenfalls bescheiden – ein winziges steinernes Fischerhaus mit einer Fläche von etwa 30 Quadratmetern. Im Naturreservat Ria Formosa gelegen, blickt es über Marschland und Dünen zum Meer. In der Nähe liegt die einstige römische Siedlung Balsa. Von Rosen erweiterte das Erdgeschoss und baute Gästezimmer und zwei Terrassen darüber. Die dekorative Ausgestaltung ist ihr zufolge ein sich ständig in Entwicklung befindlicher Prozess. Eines Abends malte sie ein Fischmotiv auf einen Schrank. „Meine Hand rutschte aus, und plötzlich hatte einer der Fische eine Zigarette im Maul!" Abgesehen von künstlerischen Missgeschicken ist ihre einzige Sorge die globale Erwärmung. „Bei Flut liegen nur einige Zentimeter zwischen dem Meer und der Türschwelle."

Previous page: A view over the marshland and dunes towards the beach. The tower-like chimney was created by a local potter.
Facing page: A view from the outside terrace into the sitting room. The fish motifs on the cupboard were painted by von Rosen.
Above: The blue door is the main entrance to the property. Cane was used for the enclosure and cotton for the seating area.
Right: Von Rosen brought the kitchen tiles back from Morocco. The traditional stool under the window is still made by hand in the Algarve region.

Pages précédente : La mer s'étend de l'autre côté du marais et des dunes. La drôle de cheminée a été réalisée par un potier local.
Page de gauche : Le salon vu depuis la terrasse. Les poissons sur le buffet ont été peints par von Rosen.
En haut : La porte d'entrée bleue de la maison. Des cloisons en jonc pour ce coin repos tapissé d'un coton à rayures blanches et bleues.
À droite : Von Rosen a rapporté le carrelage de la cuisine du Maroc. Dans la région de l'Algarve, des artisans continuent de fabriquer les tabourets traditionnels comme celui sous la fenêtre.

Vorhergehende Seiten: Blick über das Marschland und die Dünen zum Strand. Der turmähnliche Schornstein ist das Werk eines einheimischen Töpfers.
Gegenüberliegende Seite: Blick von der Außenterrasse ins Wohnzimmer. Die Fischmotive wurden von Christina gemalt.
Oben: Die blaue Tür bildet den Zugang zum Anwesen. Auf der Veranda wurde Schilfrohr für die Einfassung und blau-weiß gestreifte Baumwolle für die Sitzecke verwendet.
Rechts: Die Küchenfliesen brachte Christina von Rosen aus Marokko mit. Der traditionelle Hocker unter dem Fenster wird an der Algarve Küste immer noch in Handarbeit gefertigt.

Above: The cotton mosquito net in the guest bedroom was acquired in Amsterdam. The cotton sheets come from Greece.
Right: A flight of stairs leads from one roof terrace to another.
Facing page: In one corner of the sitting room, an old cabinet bought at a flea market, a traditional Portuguese folding chair and a stool found under a tree.

En haut : La moustiquaire en coton de la chambre d'amis vient d'Amsterdam, les draps en coton de Grèce.
À droite : Des marches relient entre elles les terrasses sur le toit.
Page de droite : Dans un coin du salon, une vieille armoire chinée sur un marché aux puces, un fauteuil pliant traditionnel portugais et un tabouret découvert sous un arbre.

Oben: Das Moskitonetz aus Baumwolle im Gästezimmer ist ein Kauf aus Amsterdam. Die Baumwoll-Bettwäsche kommt aus Griechenland.
Rechts: Eine Treppe führt von einer Dachterrasse zur anderen.
Gegenüberliegende Seite: In einer Ecke des Wohnzimmers eine alte Vitrine vom Flohmarkt, ein traditioneller portugiesischer Klappstuhl und ein unter einem Baum gefundener Hocker.

Gianna & Theodore Angelopoulos

Mykonos, Greece

Gianna Angelopoulos fut la présidente du comité d'organisation des Jeux olympiques d'Athènes en 2004. Son mari Théodore est armateur et l'un des plus grands industriels de Grèce. Ensemble, ils ont construit une série de villas perchées sur la côte sauvage et spectaculaire au sud-ouest de Mykonos. Pour les deux premières, ils ont fait appel au décorateur parisien, Alberto Pinto, lui demandant un décor élégant et de haute qualité, qui reflète la tradition architecturale de l'île. Pour la maison d'amis, Pinto a opté pour une atmosphère « plus détendue et rustique ». Chaque chambre est peinte d'un bleu différent. Dans la maison principale, le blanc domine. Partout, il a intégré des références à la mer et à la Grèce antique. La forme des canapés et des coussins évoque des galets tandis que des dieux de l'Antiquité, tels Poséidon et Apollon, ornent les murs.

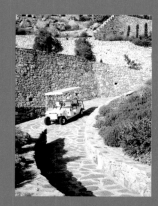

Gianna Angelopoulos was the president of the Athens 2004 Organizing Committee for the Olympic Games. Her husband, Theodore, is a leading Greek industrialist and shipping magnate. Together, they have developed a series of houses on a dramatic, rugged hillside on the southwest coast of Mykonos. For the first two, they called in Paris-based decorator Alberto Pinto and requested not only elegance and high quality, but also something that reflects the island's architectural character. For the guesthouse, Pinto opted for a "more relaxed, more rustic" ambience. There, every room has been painted a different shade of blue. In the main house, the predominant colour is white. Throughout, he integrated numerous references to both the sea and ancient Greece. The form of sofas and cushions were inspired by pebbles and images of ancient gods like Poseidon and Apollo were painted onto the walls.

Gianna Angelopoulos war Präsidentin des griechischen Organisationskomitees der Olympischen Spiele 2004 in Athen. Ihr Ehemann Theodore ist ein führender griechischer Industriemagnat und Reeder. Gemeinsam haben die beiden in dramatischer Landschaft auf einem zerklüfteten Hang an der südwestlichen Küste von Mykonos eine Reihe von Häusern gebaut. Für die ersten beiden nahmen sie die Dienste des Pariser Innenarchitekten Alberto Pinto in Anspruch. Sie wünschten etwas Elegantes, qualitativ Hochwertiges, das gleichzeitig den architektonischen Charakter der Insel widerspiegeln sollte. Beim Gästehaus plädierte Pinto für eine „eher entspannte, rustikale Atmosphäre". Dort ist jeder Raum in einem unterschiedlichen Blauton gehalten, doch im Haupthaus herrscht Weiß vor. Überall finden sich zahlreiche Anspielungen auf das Meer und das antike Griechenland. Die Sofas und Kissen orientieren sich an den Formen der Kieselsteine am Strand, während aufgemalte antike Götter wie Poseidon und Apollon von den Wänden blicken.

Previous pages: A "Sitting Bull" daybed from Lambert in one of the outdoor seating areas. The houses sit on terraces, connected by a spaghetti-like system of roads.
Above: Parasols from Kettal stand at the end of the infinity pool.
Right: One of the guesthouse's outdoor areas has been equipped with a painted wooden roof. The two rattan armchairs are Lambert's "Buster Keaton" model.

Pages précédentes : Un lit de repos « Sitting Bull » de chez Lambert dans l'un des salons extérieurs. Les maisons sont posées sur des terrasses reliées entre elles par un réseau de routes étroites et sinueuses.
En haut : Des parasols de chez Kettal devant la piscine à débordement.
À droite : Un des salons extérieurs de la maison d'amis est protégé par un toit en bois peint. Les deux fauteuils en rotin « Buster Keaton » viennent de chez Lambert.

Vorhergehende Seiten: Eine „Sitting Bull"-Chaiselongue von Lambert auf einer der Terrassen. Die Häuser liegen auf Plattformen, die durch ein Spaghetti-ähnliches System von Straßen miteinander verbunden sind.
Oben: Sonnenschirme von Kettal stehen am Ende des Infinity Pools.
Rechts: Ein gestrichenes Holzdach schmückt die Terrasse eines der Gästehäuser. Bei den beiden Rattan-Stühlen handelt es sich um das „Buster Keaton"-Modell von Lambert.

New Seaside Interiors   Gianna & Theodore Angelopoulos

Right: The figure on the wall of the dining room in the guesthouse represents Artemis. The teak table was designed by Jérôme Abel Seguin and the chairs are the "Klismos" model from Saridis.
Below: The form of the sofa and cushions in the living room of the main house was inspired by pebbles. An Antonio Citterio coffee table for Maxalto sits on a rug from El Tapisero.

À droite : Le personnage peint sur le mur de la salle à manger dans la maison des invités représente Artémis. La table en teck a été dessinée par Jérôme Abel Seguin et les chaises « Klismos » viennent de chez Saridis.
En bas : Dans le séjour de la maison principale, la forme des canapés et des coussins a été inspirée par des galets ; une table créée par Antonio Citterio pour Maxalto est posée sur un tapis d'El Tapisero.

Rechts: An der Wand des Esszimmers im Gästehaus prangt eine Darstellung der Göttin Artemis. Der Tisch aus Teakholz wurde von Jérôme Abel Seguin entworfen, die Stühle sind das Modell „Klismos" von Saridis.
Unten: Das Sofa und die Kissen im Wohnzimmer des Haupthauses beziehen sich auf die Formen von Kieselsteinen. Ein für Maxalto entworfener Beistelltisch von Antonio Citterio steht auf einem Teppich von El Tapisero.

Yorgos Zaphiriou
Serifos, Greece

Serifos, une des plus petites Cyclades, est connue pour ses chapelles blanches, ses plages et ses paysages sauvages. « C'est très aride et austère », confie, ravi, l'architecte Yorgos Zaphiriou, basé à Athènes. Il a construit sa maison d'été au sud-est de l'île avec le décorateur de théâtre Manolis Pandelidakis en s'inspirant de l'architecture des forteresses grecques. « Un ami m'a dit qu'elle lui rappelait le palais de Mycènes. » Il l'a bâtie avec les pierres extraites en creusant les fondations, afin de « donner l'impression qu'elle avait jailli du sol ». La cuisine-salle à manger, généralement remplie de monde, est le cœur de la maison. « Nous devons partager nos vies avec nos amis ; autrement, à quoi bon avoir une telle maison ? »

One of the smallest of the Cycladic islands, Serifos is known for its whitewashed chapels, beaches and rugged landscapes. "It's very harsh, very austere," opines Athens-based architect Yorgos Zaphiriou. Still, that's exactly how he likes it. His summerhouse on the southeast of the island was created in collaboration with set designer Manolis Pandelidakis. Their inspiration was the architecture of Greek fortresses. "A friend told me it reminds him of the Palace of Mycenae," states Zaphiriou. To build it, he used stones dug up on site for the foundations. "I wanted to give the impression that it had sprung from the ground," he says. Inside, the home's heart is very much the kitchen-cum-dining room, which is generally buzzing with people. "We have to share our life with friends," he asserts. "Otherwise, there's no reason to have such a house!"

Serifos, eine der kleinsten Kykladeninseln, ist bekannt für ihre weiß getünchten kleinen Kirchen, Strände und ihre raue Landschaft. „Es ist sehr schroff, sehr herb hier", meint der in Athen beheimatete Architekt Yorgos Zaphiriou. Doch gerade diese Rauheit gefällt ihm. Sein Sommerhaus im Südosten der Insel entstand in Zusammenarbeit mit dem Set-Designer Manolis Pandelidakis. Die Architektur griechischer Festungen diente ihnen als Inspiration. „Ein Freund sagte mir, das Haus erinnere ihn an den Palast von Mykene", berichtet Zaphiriou. Zum Bau verwendete er Steine, die für das Fundament an Ort und Stelle ausgegraben wurden. „Ich wollte den Eindruck vermitteln, das Gebäude sei aus dem Boden gewachsen", sagt er. Im Inneren ist der Mittelpunkt des Hauses die Wohnküche, in der es meist von Menschen wimmelt. „Wir müssen unser Leben mit Freunden teilen", bekräftigt er. „Sonst hätte es ja gar keinen Sinn, solch ein Haus zu besitzen."

Below: The master bedroom is a study in simplicity. A mosquito net hangs over a bed, which stands on blocks of stones.
Facing page: In the master suite, the bed head doubles as a stand for the stone sink. The marble column in the foreground was sculpted by Zaphiriou.

En bas : La chambre principale est une étude de simplicité. Une moustiquaire est suspendue au-dessus du lit posé sur des blocs de pierre.
Page de droite : Dans la suite principale, le dos de la tête de lit sert de support à un lavabo en pierre. La colonne en marbre au premier plan a été sculptée par Zaphiriou.

Unten: Das Schlafzimmer ist ein Muster an Schlichtheit. Ein Moskitonetz hängt über einem auf Steinblöcken stehenden Bett.
Gegenüberliegende Seite: Im Badezimmer dient das Kopfende des Bettes als Rückwand des steinernen Waschbeckens. Die kleine Marmorsäule im Vordergrund hat Zaphiriou selbst geschaffen.

Previous pages: The white chair on the platform outside the living room was originally used on cruise ships. The uninhabited island of Vous can be seen beyond the infinity pool.
Above: The kitchen/dining room is the soul of the house. Eero Saarinen's "Tulip" chairs are grouped around an iroko table designed by Zaphiriou. The kitchen counter is made from concrete.

Pages précédentes : Une chaise longue de paquebot en bois blanc sur le palier devant le séjour. Depuis la piscine à débordement, on peut contempler l'île déserte de Vous.
En haut : La cuisine-salle à manger est l'âme de la maison. Les sièges « Tulip » d'Eero Saarinen entourent une table en iroko dessinée par Zaphiriou. Le comptoir de la cuisine est en béton.

Vorhergehende Seiten: Der weiße Stuhl auf der Plattform vor dem Wohnzimmer ist ein typischer Deckchair, wie er auf Kreuzfahrtschiffen üblich ist. Die unbewohnte Insel Vous taucht hinter dem Infinity Pool aus dem Meer.
Oben: Die Wohnküche ist die Seele des Hauses. Eero Saarinens „Tulip"-Stühle sind um einen vom Zaphiriou entworfenen Tisch aus Irokoholz gruppiert. Die Arbeitsplatte besteht aus Beton.

New Seaside Interiors   Yorgos Zaphiriou

Alan Wanzenberg

Fire Island, New York

L'architecte Alan Wanzenberg, basé à New York, n'a pas une mais deux maisons sur Fire Island. Ocean House, qui compte quatre chambres, appartenait autrefois au créateur Perry Ellis. Bay House, plus petite, a été construite sur le site d'une structure quasiment identique détruite par un incendie en 1992. Reliées par une promenade en cèdre, elles sont merveilleusement isolées, le terrain tout autour appartenant aux parcs nationaux. Donc, pas de voisins. Selon Wanzenberg, Ocean House est « extravertie, claire, légère, tandis que Bay House est plus sombre, mélancolique ». Toutes deux sont aménagées avec des éléments encastrés et un assortiment de meubles français des années 50 et néoclassiques suédois. Il y règne une atmosphère décontractée. « Il n'y a pas grand-chose à faire ici. J'ai pris goût à ces longues périodes de temps déstructuré. »

New York-based architect Alan Wanzenberg has not one... but two houses on Fire Island. The four-bedroom Ocean House used to belong to fashion designer Perry Ellis. The smaller Bay House was built on the site of an almost identical structure, which burnt in a 1992 fire. Linked by a cedar boardwalk, they are wonderfully remote. The land on either side belongs to the National Parks Service... which means no neighbours. According to Wanzenberg, the Ocean House "is extroverted, lighter, brighter". The Bay House, meanwhile, is "darker, a bit moodier". Both are decorated with a mix of post-War French furniture, Swedish Neoclassical pieces and a number of built-in elements. Life there is apparently wonderfully laid-back. "The options for doing things are quite limited," he rejoices. "What I've come to enjoy are the long periods of unstructured time."

Der New Yorker Architekt Alan Wanzenberg besitzt nicht nur eines, sondern zwei Häuser auf Fire Island. Das sogenannte Ocean House mit vier Schlafzimmern gehörte zuvor dem Modeschöpfer Perry Ellis. Das kleinere Bay House genannte entstand auf dem Grundriss eines nahezu identischen, 1992 abgebrannten Bauwerks. Beide sind mit einem Holzsteg aus Zedernholz verbunden und wunderbar einsam gelegen. Das Land zu beiden Seiten gehört der Nationalen Parkverwaltung – es gibt also keine Nachbarn. Laut Wanzenberg ist das Ocean House „extrovertierter, leichter, heller", das Bay House dagegen „düsterer, ein wenig melancholisch". Beide sind mit einer Mischung aus französischen Möbeln der Nachkriegszeit, schwedischen klassizistischen Stücken und Einbauelementen eingerichtet. Das Leben scheint dort auf wundersame Weise stehen geblieben oder gar rückständig zu sein. „Die Möglichkeiten zur Beschäftigung sind hier ziemlich begrenzt", strahlt der Besitzer. „Ich genieße die langen Phasen unverplanter Zeit."

Left: A Swedish Neoclassical sofa, an Arts & Crafts table and two Charlotte Perriand chairs in the Ocean House living room.
Below: A surfboard is propped up against the wall in one of the Ocean House bedrooms.
Facing page: A French 1950s chair stands in front of an antique Swedish chest in the master bedroom of the Ocean House. The checked woollen blanket dates from the early 20th century.

À gauche : Dans le séjour d'Ocean House, un canapé néoclassique suédois, une table Arts & Craft et deux fauteuils de Charlotte Perriand.
En bas : Dans l'une des chambres d'Ocean House, une planche de surf posée contre un mur.
Page de droite : Dans la chambre principale d'Ocean House, une chaise française des années 50 devant un vieux secrétaire suédois. La couverture à carreaux en laine date du début du XXᵉ siècle.

Links: Im Wohnzimmer des Ocean House stehen ein schwedisches klassizistisches Sofa, ein Tisch aus der Arts-and-Crafts-Bewegung und zwei Charlotte-Perriand-Stühle.
Unten: Ein Surfbrett an der Wand eines Schlafzimmers im Ocean House.
Gegenüberliegende Seite: Im Ocean House steht im Elternschlafzimmer ein französischer Stuhl aus den 1950er-Jahren vor einer antiken schwedischen Kommode. Die Wolldecke mit Karomuster stammt aus dem frühen 20. Jahrhundert.

Previous pages: Two armchairs from Dominique stand in front of the fireplace in the Ocean House living room. The other chairs are by Charlotte Perriand and the two blue lamps from Fantoni.

Pages précédentes : Dans le séjour d'Ocean House, deux fauteuils de Dominique devant la cheminée. Les autres sièges sont de Charlotte Perriand et les deux lampes bleues viennent de chez Fantoni.

Vorhergehende Seiten: Im Ocean House stehen zwei Lehnstühle von Dominique vor dem Kamin im Wohnzimmer. Die anderen Stühle sind von Charlotte Perriand, die beiden blauen Stehlampen von Fantoni.

New Seaside Interiors   Alan Wanzenberg

Facing page: A Mathieu Matégot light fixture hangs above a seating area in the Bay House bedroom.
Above: Two Paul László chairs face an Edward Durell Stone sofa in the Bay House sitting room. The rug is Moroccan.
Right: Wanzenberg designed the bed in the Bay House from fir.

Page de gauche : Un luminaire de Mathieu Matégot est suspendu au-dessus du coin salon de la chambre de Bay House.
En haut : Dans le salon de Bay House, une paire de fauteuils de Paul László face à un canapé d'Edward Durell Stone. Le tapis est marocain.
À droite : Wanzenberg a dessiné le lit en sapin de la chambre de Bay House.

Gegenüberliegende Seite: Eine Deckenlampe von Mathieu Matégot hängt im Bay House über einer Sitzgruppe im Schlafzimmer.
Oben: Im Bay House stehen im Wohnzimmer zwei Stühle von Paul László einem Sofa von Edward Durell Stone gegenüber. Der Teppich ist marokkanisch.
Rechts: Wanzenberg entwarf das Bett im Bay House aus Kiefernholz.

Annabelle Selldorf

Long Island, New York

L'architecte Annabelle Selldorf cherchait une maison de week-end qui offre une rupture avec son quotidien. « Je la voulais simple pour me reposer des 'complications' de mes clients. » Parmi ses projets en date, le musée Neue Galerie à Manhattan, les boutiques phares internationales d'Abercrombie & Fitch et un atelier pour Jeff Koons. La bâtisse construite en 1957 qu'elle a dénichée dans la Gardiner's Bay à Long Island est on ne peut plus humble. « C'est une maison très rudimentaire », confie-t-elle, mais elle a été séduite par sa belle terrasse en bois et son site « incroyablement romantique ». Elle apprécie également le noir absolu qui y règne la nuit. « Long Island n'est qu'à deux pas de New York mais, ici, c'est le dépaysement absolu. Je m'y sens vraiment en vacances. »

When architect Annabelle Selldorf went looking for a weekend home, she insisted that it offer a break from her daily life. "I wanted something uncomplicated", she says, "because I'm always dealing with clients' complications." Among her projects to date are the Neue Galerie museum in Manhattan, international flagships for Abercrombie & Fitch and a studio for artist Jeff Koons. The 1957 house she found on Long Island's Gardiner's Bay is certainly rather less high-profile. "I'm sure it was rather inexpensive because it's a very primitive house," she notes. That said, she was seduced by its beautiful deck and its "unbelievably romantic" location. She also loves the fact that, at night, it gets pitch black. "It's astonishing just how much of a break it can be," she remarks. "Long Island is so close to New York. Yet, it's like going on a vacation."

Als die Architektin Annabelle Selldorf nach einem Wochenendhaus suchte, stand für sie fest, dass es ihr eine Pause von ihrem täglichen Leben bieten müsse. „Ich wollte etwas Unkompliziertes", sagt sie, „denn die Wünsche meiner Kunden zu erfüllen ist kompliziert genug." Zu ihren bislang ausgeführten Projekten gehören das Museum Neue Galerie in Manhattan, die internationalen Flagshipstores für Abercrombie & Fitch und ein Atelier für den Künstler Jeff Koons. Das Haus mit Baujahr 1957, das sie in der Gardiner's Bay auf Long Island fand, ist zweifellos weniger hochklassig. „Es war ziemlich preiswert, weil es ein sehr einfaches Haus ist", meint sie. Doch war sie von seiner schönen Terrasse und der „unglaublich romantischen" Lage bezaubert. Auch dass es dort in der Nacht stockdunkel wird, begeistert sie. „Es ist erstaunlich, wie groß der Unterschied sein kann", sagt sie. „Long Island liegt so nahe bei New York. Und doch ist es, als wäre man in Urlaub."

Left and below: The all-white master bedroom remains serene and zen. The marble bathroom is the most luxurious room in the house.

À gauche et en bas : La chambre toute blanche est sereine et zen. La salle de bains en marbre est la pièce la plus luxueuse de la maison.

Links und unten: Das ganz in Weiß gehaltene Schlafzimmer strahlt eine heiter-gelassene Zen-Stimmung aus. Das Marmorbad ist der luxuriöseste Raum des Hauses.

Previous pages: Simple tables and chairs from Crate & Barrel stand on the back deck. Two George Nelson benches have been reupholstered in a white canvas in the living room.
Facing page: Selldorf shipped the rough-hewn table from England. The chairs are the "Brno" model by Ludwig Mies van der Rohe.

Pages précédentes : Une table et des chaises toutes simples de chez Crate & Barrel sur la terrasse derrière la maison. Dans le séjour, deux banquettes de George Nelson ont été retapissées de toile blanche.
Page de gauche : Selldorf a fait venir la table en bois brut d'Angleterre. Elle est entourée de fauteuils « Brno » de Ludwig Mies van der Rohe.

Vorhergehende Seiten: Schlichte Tische und Stühle von Crate & Barrel auf der hinteren Terrasse. Im Wohnzimmer stehen zwei George-Nelson-Sofas, die mit weißem Leinen neu bezogen wurden.
Gegenüberliegende Seite: Annabelle ließ den grob gezimmerten Tisch per Schiff aus England kommen. Die Stühle daran sind das „Brno"-Modell von Ludwig Mies van der Rohe.

Lisa Perry

Sag Harbor, New York

C'est la vue qui a fait craquer la styliste de mode Lisa Perry. « Depuis la porte d'entrée, on voit jusqu'à la mer ». Située sur un des points les plus élevés des Hamptons, sa demeure de six chambres domine Noyac Bay. Construite en 1910 par le navigateur mondain Reginald Barclay, la maison devint un monastère après la guerre. La trouvant trop traditionnelle à son goût, Perry a fait appel au cabinet d'architectes 1100: Architect et aux décorateurs Tony Ingrao et Alexia Kondylis. La façade en briques a été enduite de stuc et l'intérieur transformé en « paradis de couleurs primaires ». Les murs blancs sont égayés par les explosions de tons vifs des accessoires et de l'art minimaliste géométrique. « J'ai une aversion pour les couleurs qui ne sont pas pures », déclare Perry. « J'aime les ambiances joyeuses qui vous mettent le sourire aux lèvres. »

For fashion designer Lisa Perry, it was all about the view. "You walk in the front door and can see through to the water," she asserts. Situated on one of the highest points in the Hamptons, her six-bedroom house enjoys an expansive vista of Noyac Bay. Built in 1910 by socialite and yachtsman Reginald Barclay, it later served as a post-war monastery. To revamp the oh-too-traditional pile, Perry enlisted the help of the 1100: Architect firm and interior designers Tony Ingrao and Alexia Kondylis. The original brick façade was re-covered with stucco. The inside has been called a "primary-colour paradise". The walls may be white, but accessories and minimalist geometric art make the place pop with bright hues. As Perry says: "I have a real aversion to colours that aren't pure. I like a happy environment. A place where people walk in and smile!"

Der Modedesignerin Lisa Perry ging es allein um die Aussicht. „Man tritt durch die Eingangstüre ins Haus und kann direkt bis zum Wasser schauen", stellt sie zufrieden fest. Auf einem der höchsten Punkte in den Hamptons angesiedelt, gewährt ihr Haus mit sechs Schlafzimmern einen weiten Blick auf die Noyac Bay. 1910 von dem in Gesellschaftskreisen bekannten Yachtbesitzer Reginald Barclay erbaut, diente es nach dem Krieg als Kloster. Um das allzu traditionelle Gebäude aufzupolieren, gewann Lisa Perry die unschätzbare Hilfe der Innenarchitekten Tony Ingrao und Alexia Kondylis sowie deren Firma 1100: Architect. Die ursprüngliche Ziegelfassade wurde verputzt, und das Innere galt bald als „Primärfarben-Paradies". Die Wände mögen zwar weiß sein, aber Accessoires und minimalistische geometrische Kunst lassen das Hausinnere vor knallig-bunten Farbtönen überquellen. Wie Lisa sagt: „Ich habe eine echte Aversion gegen Farben, die nicht rein sind. Ich mag eine fröhliche Umgebung, ein Haus, das die Leute betreten und lächeln."

Facing page: Bright red sculptures by artist Zhu Jinshi are dotted around the garden.
Above: More visual drama is provided outside by the one-off Robert Indiana mosaic table and the Alexia Kondylis-designed custom sofas.
Right: A Niki de Saint Phalle sculpture surveys the pool.

Page de gauche : Des sculptures rouge vif de Zhu Jinshi parsèment le jardin.
En haut : Sur la terrasse, un autre puissant effet visuel grâce à la table en mosaïque de Robert Indiana, un exemplaire unique, et aux canapés réalisés sur mesure par Alexia Kondylis.
À droite : Une sculpture de Niki de Saint Phalle surveille la piscine.

Gegenüberliegende Seite: In hellem Rot erstrahlende Skulpturen des Künstlers Zhu Jinshi sind im Garten verteilt.
Oben: Weitere dramatische visuelle Akzente im Freien setzen der Mosaiktisch von Robert Indiana und die maßgefertigten Sofas von Alexia Kondylis.
Rechts: Eine Skulptur von Niki de Saint Phalle blickt über den Pool.

Previous pages: Perry installed a plethora of George Nelson's "Bubble" lamps above the Tucker Robbins dining table and Eero Saarinen chairs. The multicoloured oil painting on the back wall is by Karl Benjamin.
Above: Among the artworks in the sitting room are oils by Frank Stella (left) and Leon Polk Smith (back wall). The sectional sofas were custom designed by Tony Ingrao.
Right: A work by Tadaaki Kuwayama hangs above a red Robert Wilson-designed bench in the entry hall.

Pages précédentes : Perry a suspendu une armée de luminaires « Bubble » de George Nelson au-dessus d'une table de Tucker Robbins et de chaises d'Eero Saarinen. La peinture à l'huile multicolore sur le mur du fond est une œuvre de Karl Benjamin.
En haut : Dans le salon, des œuvres de Frank Stella (à gauche) et de Leon Polk Smith (mur du fond). Les canapés modulaires ont été réalisés sur mesure par Tony Ingrao.
À droite : Dans l'entrée, une œuvre de Tadaaki Kuwayama au-dessus d'un banc rouge de Robert Wilson.

Vorhergehende Seiten: Lisa installierte eine Unmenge von George Nelsons „Bubble"-Lampen über dem Esstisch von Tucker Robbins und den Stühlen von Eero Saarinen. Das bunt gestreifte Ölgemälde an der Rückwand ist von Karl Benjamin.
Oben: Unter den Kunstwerken im Wohnzimmer befinden sich Ölgemälde von Frank Stella (links) und Leon Polk Smith (Rückwand). Die zusammensetzbaren Sofaelemente wurden von Tony Ingrao maßgefertigt.
Rechts: Ein Werk von Tadaaki Kuwayama hängt über einer roten, von Robert Wilson entworfenen Sitzbank in der Eingangshalle.

New Seaside Interiors   Lisa Perry

Right and below: In the master bedroom, Gaetano Pesce's iconic "Donna" chair and ottoman from the Up series stand on a platform in the master bedroom. The ten-foot circular bed was custom-made and the pendant lights were designed by Tom Dixon.

*À **droite et en bas** :* Dans la chambre principale, le célèbre fauteuil et pouf « Donna » de la série Up de Gaetano Pesce est posé sur une estrade. Le lit circulaire de 3 m de diamètre a été réalisé sur mesure. Les luminaires suspendus au plafond sont de Tom Dixon.

Rechts und unten: Im Hauptschlafzimmer steht die Stuhlikone „Donna" mit Ottomane aus der Up-Serie von Gaetano Pesce auf einer Plattform. Das Rundbett mit einem Durchmesser von 3 Metern wurde nach Maß angefertigt, und die Hängelampen sind Entwürfe von Tom Dixon.

Facing page: The three primary colours come together in the kitchen. The blue units were custom-made, and the apple and lemon are artworks created by Perry. A "Taraxacum" light from Flos hangs over the central island. The stools are the "Spoon" model, created by Antonio Citterio and Toan Nguyen for Kartell.

Page de droite : Les trois couleurs primaires se rejoignent dans la cuisine. Les éléments bleus ont été réalisés sur mesure. La pomme et le citron sont des œuvres de Perry. Un lustre « Taraxacum » de chez Flos est suspendu au-dessus de l'îlot central. Les tabourets « Spoon » ont été créés par Antonio Citterio et Toan Nguyen pour Kartell.

Gegenüberliegende Seite: In der Küche treffen die drei Primärfarben aufeinander. Die blauen Einheiten wurden nach Maß angefertigt, und der Apfel und die Zitrone sind von Lisa Perry geschaffene Kunstwerke. Eine „Taraxacum"-Lampe von Flos hängt über der zentralen Insel. Die Hocker sind das für Kartell entworfene „Spoon"-Modell von Antonio Citterio und Toan Nguyen.

Above: The table is also set on the dining-room wall, thanks to artist Alex Hay's 1964 fibreglass sculpture, "Egg on Plate with Knife, Fork, and Spoon".
Right: Verner Panton's "Fun 1 DM" chandeliers shimmer above Alexia Kondylis-designed red benches in the upstairs hallway.

En haut : Dans la salle à manger, le couvert a également été dressé sur le mur. Cette sculpture en fibre de verre d'Alex Hay, datant de 1964, s'intitule « Egg on Plate with Knife, Fork, and Spoon ».
À droite : Dans le couloir à l'étage, deux lustres « Fun 1 DM » de Verner Panton scintillent au-dessus de bancs rouges dessinés par Alexia Kondylis.

Oben: Auch an der Wand des Speisezimmers ist der Tisch gedeckt – dank der Fiberglas-Skulptur des Künstlers Alex Hay aus dem Jahr 1964 mit dem Titel „Egg on Plate with Knife, Fork and Spoon".
Rechts: Verner Pantons „Fun 1 DM"-Lampen hängen über den roten von Alexia Kondylis entworfenen Bänken in der Halle der oberen Etage.

New Seaside Interiors   Lisa Perry

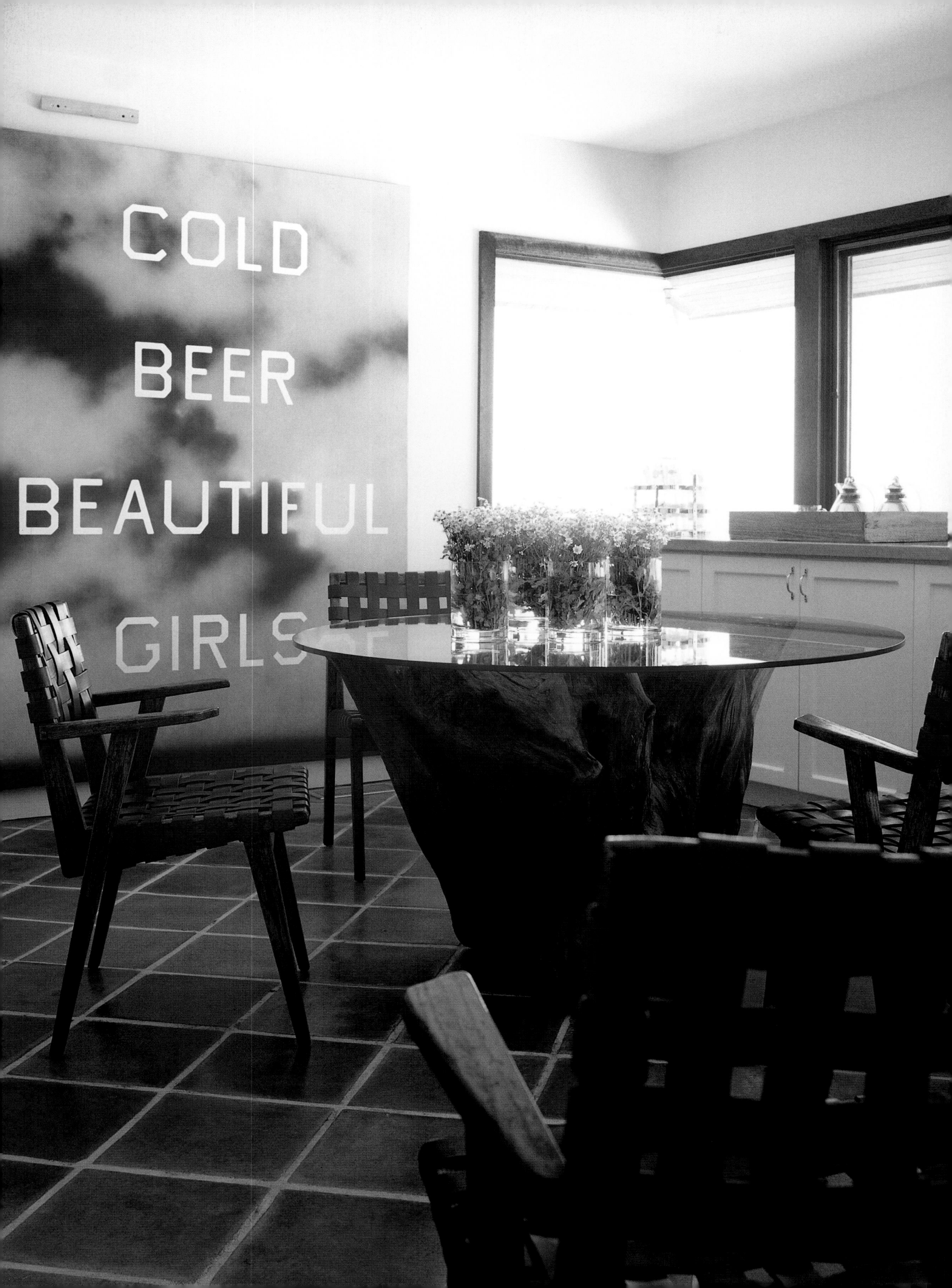
COLD
BEER
BEAUTIFUL
GIRLS

Danielle & David Ganek

Southampton, New York

Pour Joe Nahem, de Fox-Nahem Design, les Hamptons sont un lieu "à part". « Un endroit si tranquille près d'une métropole comme New York, c'est exceptionnel. » Toutefois, ce projet pour les collectionneurs Danielle et David Ganek et leurs trois enfants ne fut pas de tout repos. « Ils nous ont confié la maison en avril et la voulaient prête pour l'été. » Située sur une péninsule, la structure assez simple jouit de vues imprenables sur l'océan et la baie de Shinnecock. Avec Tom Fox, aujourd'hui disparu, Nahem a installé un nouveau toit de bardeaux et agrandi le hall pour créer une double hauteur sous plafond. L'intérieur, aménagé avec des meubles vintages et des pièces sur mesure, n'a rien d'une maison de plage, si ce n'est pour les tissus robustes. « Les propriétaires voulaient néanmoins qu'on puisse s'asseoir avec son maillot mouillé. »

For Joe Nahem of Fox-Nahem Design, The Hamptons is "a very special place. It's unusual to have somewhere so tranquil next to a huge city like New York." Still, this project for art collectors Danielle and David Ganek and their three children was anything but leisurely. "We got the house in April and they wanted it by the summer," recalls Nahem. The structure may be simple enough. The location, however, is truly spectacular. Situated on a peninsula, it offers views of both the ocean and Shinnecock Bay. Working with the late Tom Fox, Nahem put on a new shingle roof and extended the entry hall to create a double-height space. Inside, vintage pieces and custom creations were assembled for a decidedly un-beachy look. Sturdy fabrics, however, remained a must. "The owners still wanted people to be able to sit down in a wet bathing suit."

Für Joe Nahem von Fox-Nahem Design sind die Hamptons „ein ganz besonderer Ort. Die Existenz eines so ruhevollen Fleckchens Erde in der Nähe einer riesigen Stadt wie New York ist ungewöhnlich." Für die Kunstsammler Danielle und David Ganek und ihre drei Kinder war dieses Projekt zunächst nicht mit viel Ruhe verbunden. „Wir bekamen den Auftrag für das Haus im April, und sie wollten es schon im Sommer nutzen", erinnert sich Nahem. Das Gebäude mag einfach sein, doch die Lage ist spektakulär. Auf einer Halbinsel gelegen, bietet das Haus Ausblicke auf den Atlantik und die Shinnecock Bay. In Zusammenarbeit mit dem inzwischen verstorbenen Tom Fox schuf Nahem ein neues Schindeldach und baute die Eingangshalle zu einem doppelgeschossigen Raum aus. Die Zusammenstellung von Vintage-Objekten und maßgefertigten Möbeln im Inneren strahlt entschieden keine Strand-Atmosphäre aus. Dennoch waren strapazierfähige Stoffe bei alledem ein Muss. „Die Besitzer legten Wert darauf, dass die Leute sich auch in einem nassen Badeanzug hinsetzen konnten."

Previous pages: *Ed Ruscha's 1993 painting "Cold Beer Beautiful Girls" hangs behind a glass-topped tree-trunk table in the kitchen.*
Above: *The mahogany deck affords sweeping views of Shinnecock Bay. The Petal Coffee table was originally designed by Richard Schultz in 1960.*
Right: *Richard Schultz dining chairs are grouped around a custom Fox-Nahem table made from anodized powder-coated metal.*

Pages précédentes : *Dans la cuisine, une toile d'Ed Ruscha de 1993, « Cold Beer Beautiful Girls », est accrochée devant une table réalisée avec une souche d'arbre et un plateau en verre.*
Ci-dessus : *Depuis la terrasse en acajou, on a une vue panoramique sur la baie de Shinnecock. La table basse « Petal » a été désinée par Richard Schultz en 1960.*
À droite : *Des chaises de Richard Schultz autour d'une table réalisée spécialement par Fox-Nahem en métal poudré et anodisé.*

Vorhergehende Seite: *Ed Ruschas Gemälde „Cold Beer Beautiful Girls" (Kaltes Bier, schöne Mädchen) aus dem Jahr 1993 hängt in der Küche hinter einem Glastisch mit einem Baumstumpf als Sockel.*
Oben: *Die Mahagoni-Terrasse bietet weite Ausblicke auf die Shinnecock Bay. Der „Petal"-Beistelltisch wurde von Richard Schultz 1960 entworfen.*
Rechts: *Die Esstischstühle von Richard Schultz sind um einen von Fox-Nahem maßgefertigten Tisch mit einer eloxierten Metalloberfläche gruppiert.*

New Seaside Interiors   Danielle & David Ganek

Right: A McKinnon and Harris Twenties Tennis Umpire Chair overlooks the pool at the side of the house. The chaise lounges are by Richard Schultz.
Below: A George Nelson Bubble lamp hangs above a George Nakashima table and oak and leather chairs from Waldo's Designs in the dining room.
Following pages: Two photos from Rineke Dijkstra's "Beach Series" hang in the double-height entry hall. The vintage chandelier is the "Fun 3DM" model by Verner Panton. The Anish Kapoor sculpture is entitled "Blood".

À droite : Une chaise d'arbitre des années 20 de chez McKinnon & Harris domine la piscine située sur le flanc de la maison. Les chaises longues sont de Richard Schultz.
Ci-dessous : Dans la salle à manger, un luminaire « Bubble » de George Nelson au-dessus d'une table de George Nakashima et de chaises en chêne et cuir provenant de Waldo's Design.
Pages suivantes : Dans le haut vestibule, deux photos de la série Beach de Rineke Dijkstra. Le chandelier vintage « Fun 3 DM » est de Verner Panton. La sculpture d'Anish Kapoor s'intitule « Blood ».

Rechts: Ein Tennis-Schiedsrichterstuhl von McKinnon und Harris Twenties steht am Pool des Hauses. Die Liegen sind von Richard Schultz.
Unten: Eine „Bubble"-Lampe von George Nelson hängt im Esszimmer über einem George-Nakashima-Tisch samt Eichenholzstühlen mit Ledergeflecht von Waldo's Designs.
Folgende Seiten: Zwei Fotos aus Rineke Dijkstras „Beach Series" hängen in der sich über zwei Geschosse erstreckenden Eingangshalle. Der Vintage-Kronleuchter ist das „Fun 3 DM"-Modell von Verner Panton. Die Skulptur von Anish Kapoor trägt den Titel „Blood".

Above: *A sweeping Vladimir Kagan sofa dominates the living room. The two ebonised ash chairs are by Jean Royère. The artwork on the left is "The Intersection Series: Person with Accordion/Seascape" by John Baldessari.*
Right: *A Warren Platner lounge chair and a custom Fox-Nahem sectional sofa in the family room.*
Facing page: *A 1950s free-form coffee table from Galerie de Beyrie sits on a sturdy goatskin rug in the living room.*

Ci-dessus : *Un canapé tout en courbes de Vladimir Kagan domine le séjour. Les deux fauteuils en frêne teinté en noir d'ébène sont de Jean Royère. L'œuvre de John Baldessari sur la gauche s'intitule « The Intersection Series : Person with Accordion/Seascape ».*
À droite : *Dans le petit salon, un fauteuil de repos de Warren Platner et un canapé modulaire conçu spécialement par Fox-Nahem.*
Page de droite : *Dans le séjour, une table basse des années 50 aux formes fluides venant de la Galerie de Beyrie sur un robuste tapis en poils de chèvre.*

Oben: *Ein geschwungenes Vladimir-Kagan-Sofa dominiert das Wohnzimmer. Die beiden schwarz gebeizten Sessel aus Eschenholz sind von Jean Royère. Das Kunstwerk zur Linken – „The Intersection Series: Person with Accordion/Seascape" – ist von John Baldessari.*
Rechts: *Ein Warren-Platner-Sessel und ein von Fox-Nahem maßgefertigtes Sofa im Familienzimmer.*
Gegenüberliegende Seite: *Im Wohnzimmer steht ein organisch geformter Sofatisch aus den 1950er-Jahren von der Galerie de Beyrie auf einem strapazierfähigen Teppich aus Ziegenfell.*

New Seaside Interiors   Danielle & David Ganek

Shore Chic

Martha's Vineyard,
Massachusetts

« Même sous une tente, je serais heureuse à Martha's Vineyard », confie la propriétaire de cette grande demeure qui n'a rien de sommaire, dominant la mer à Edgartown. Son architecte Mark Ferguson l'a construite comme si elle avait toujours été là, avec des plafonds et des avant-toits de guingois ; la décoratrice Paula Perlini avait pour mission de créer une atmosphère très informelle. « Ils voulaient un endroit sans façons où se détendre », explique-t-elle. Elle a opté pour le côté pratique du crin végétal et du bambou qui « convient bien au bord de la mer car il supporte l'humidité de l'air ». (On remarquera la table de jeux dans la bibliothèque et le tabouret de style chinois dans le séjour). Le thème marin se retrouve, entre autres, dans les imprimés à coquillages et la vieille sirène en bois au pied de l'escalier.

"I could live in a tent on Martha's Vineyard and be happy." So says the owner of something rather grander – a six-bedroom house in Edgartown. The aim of the building's architect Mark Ferguson was to create something that looks as if it had always been there. Inside, ceilings and eaves are deliberately wonky. The brief given to decorator Paula Perlini was for something very informal. "They wanted to be able to kick their shoes off and put their feet up," she says. She used practical seagrass and numerous touches of bamboo (note the games table in the library and the Chinese-style stool in the living room). "Bamboo works well at the beach because it likes the moisture in the air," she opines. There are also shell motifs on fabrics and other quirky nautical touches. Among them, an old wooden mermaid at the foot of the stairs!

„Auf Martha's Vineyard wäre ich auch in einem Zelt glücklich." Das sagt der Besitzer von etwas weit Größerem – einem Haus mit sechs Schlafzimmern in Edgartown. Ziel des verantwortlichen Architekten Mark Ferguson war es, ein Bauwerk zu kreieren, das aussieht, als hätte es schon immer hier gestanden. Die Decken und Simse im Inneren verlaufen absichtlich etwas krumm und schief. Die Dekorateurin Paula Perlini hatte viele Freiheiten, ihr wurde lediglich vorgegeben, etwas ganz Zwangloses zu schaffen. „Sie wollten es bequem haben, ihre Schuhe ausziehen und die Füße hochlegen können", sagt sie. So verwendete sie Seegras und viele Bambus-Akzente (siehe den Spieltisch in der Bibliothek und den chinesischen Hocker im Wohnzimmer). „Bambus eignet sich gut für den Strand, weil er die Luftfeuchtigkeit liebt", meint sie. Dazu gibt es Muschelmotive auf Stoffen und andere verspielte nautische Akzente, darunter die alte Holzstatue einer Meerjungfrau auf dem Treppenabsatz.

Left: The hand-hooked rug in the mud room has nautical references.
Below: A chair in one of the guest bedrooms has been upholstered in a seashell fabric from Kravet. Perlini painted the two Louis J. Solomon beds white.

À gauche : Le tapis crocheté à la main dans la remise est décoré de motifs nautiques.
En bas : Dans une des chambres d'amis, une chaise a été tapissée d'un tissu imprimé de coquillages de Kravet. Perlini a peint en blanc les deux lits de Louis J. Solomon.

Links: Der handgeknüpfte Teppich im Abstellraum ist mit nautischen Elementen verziert.
Unten: Ein Stuhl in einem der Gästezimmer wurde mit einem muschelbedruckten Stoff von Kravet bezogen. Perlini strich die beiden Betten von Louis J. Solomon weiß.

Previous pages: The house offers a view of the Edgartown Harbor lighthouse, dating from 1938; a teak table and chairs from Barlow Tyrie in the outdoor dining area; a ship's figurehead in the form of a mermaid and a vintage fire bucket stand at the bottom of the stairs; in the library is a bamboo games table; in the sitting room, white chairs from Louis J. Solomon and an antique sofa stand on a rug designed by Elizabeth Eakins.
Facing page: The owner likes to fill the house with informal floral arrangement. Here, a casual bunch of Cosmos flowers.

Pages précédentes : La maison jouit d'une vue sur le phare d'Edgartown Harbor, construit en 1938 ; dans la salle à manger extérieure, une table et des chaises en teck de chez Barlow Tyrie ; une figure de proue en forme de sirène et un ancien seau d'incendie au pied de l'escalier ; dans la bibliothèque, une table de jeux en bambou ; dans le salon, des fauteuils blancs de Louis J. Solomon et un canapé ancien sur un tapis dessiné par Elizabeth Eakins.
Page de gauche : La propriétaire aime remplir la maison de charmants bouquets trout simples, ici des cosmos.

Vorhergehende Seiten: Das Haus gewährt Ausblick auf den Leuchtturm aus dem Jahr 1938 im Hafen von Edgartown. Ein Teakholztisch und Stühle von Barlow Tyrie für den Essbereich auf der Terrasse; eine Gallionsfigur in Gestalt einer Meerjungfrau und ein alter Feuerlöscheimer auf dem Treppenabsatz; in der Bibliothek ein Spieltisch aus Bambus; im Wohnzimmer stehen weiße Stühle von Louis J. Solomon und ein antikes Sofa auf einem von Elizabeth Eakins entworfenen Teppich.
Gegenüberliegende Seite: Der Besitzer liebt es, das Haus mit zwanglosen Blumen-Arrangements zu füllen. Hier ein lockerer Strauß von Kosmee-Blüten.

Barbara Becker

Miami, Florida

"I love contrasts," states actress and fashion designer Barbara Becker. They are certainly in evidence at the house she shares with her sons Noah and Elias (their father is tennis legend Boris). Situated on one of the Venetian Islands, the 1933 red-brick structure looks perfectly demure from the outside. Inside, however, it's lively, fun and wonderfully glamorous. Working with Oscar Glottman, Becker created a décor largely inspired by the 1960s and 1970s. She also filled the house with 17 chandeliers, one of which bears the name "Liberace". "It's so over-the-top," she explains. In the backyard are mango, papaya and banana trees (the former owner was director of the Miami Botanical Garden). There's also the ocean. "I grew up in Germany far from the sea," she asserts. "It's always been a fantasy to live by the water. So, this is a dream come true."

Previous pages: *A huge amethyst, mounted on legs, stands in front of a curtain of Swarovski crystals in the entrance hall.*
Facing page: *The Golden Retriever Chui stands on the basketball court in front of the house designed in 1933 by architect Russell Pancoast.*
Above: *Owner Barbara Becker in a yoga position by the pool. On the right is Wendell Castle's "Molar" chair. The foam rubber foot standing at the edge of the ocean was created by Gaetano Pesce.*
Right: *A view from the entrance hall into Becker's office. The Eames rocking chair stands in front of a work by Michelangelo Pistoletto.*

Pages précédentes : *Dans l'entrée, une immense améthyste montée sur pieds se dresse devant un rideau en cristaux de Swarovski.*
Page de gauche : *Chui, le golden retriever, monte la garde sur le terrain de basket devant la maison construite en 1933 par l'architecte Russell Pancoast.*
En haut : *Barbara Becker faisant son yoga devant la piscine. À droite, un fauteuil « Molar » de Wendell Castle. Le pied en mousse de caoutchouc au bord de l'océan est de Gaetano Pesce.*
À droite : *Le bureau de Becker vu depuis l'entrée. Sous une œuvre de Michelangelo Pistoletto, un rocking-chair des Eames.*

Vorhergehende Seiten: *Ein riesiger, auf Beinen ruhender Amethyst steht vor einem Vorhang aus Swarovski-Kristallen in der Eingangshalle.*
Gegenüberliegende Seite: *Der Golden Retriever Chui auf dem Basketballplatz vor dem Haus, das der Architekt Russell Pancoast 1933 entworfen hat.*
Oben: *Die Eigentümerin Barbara Becker bei einer Yoga-Übung am Pool. Rechts steht Wendell Castles „Molar"-Stuhl. Der Fuß aus Schaumstoff zwischen Pool und Ozean wurde von Gaetano Pesce entworfen.*
Rechts: *Ein Blick aus der Eingangshalle in Barbaras Büro. Der Eames-Schaukelstuhl steht vor einem Werk von Michelangelo Pistoletto.*

Above: The mood in the dining room is one of high glamour. The walls are covered with Flavor Paper's "Flower of Love" and the floor with a brightly dyed Turkish rug. The pink chandelier above the Eero Saarinen table and chairs is made from Murano glass.
Right: In the kitchen, the sober, wooden table and benches by E15 contrast with the flashy, metallic wall installation.

En haut : Du grand glamour dans la salle à manger. Les murs sont tapissés de papier peint « Flower of Love » de chez Flavor Paper. Au sol, un tapis turc teint en rose vif. Le lustre rose au-dessus de la table et des chaises d'Eero Saarinen est en verre de Murano.
À droite : Dans la cuisine, la table et les bancs en bois sobres de E15 contrastent avec l'étincelante installation murale en métal.

Oben: Das Esszimmer wirkt hochglamourös. Die Wände sind mit „Flower of Love"-Tapeten von Flavor Paper und der Boden mit einem leuchtend pink gefärbten, türkischen Teppich bedeckt. Der rosafarbene Kronleuchter über dem Eero-Saarinen-Tisch samt Stühlen wurde aus Murano-Glas gefertigt.
Rechts: In der Küche kontrastieren der schlichte Holztisch und die Bänken von E15 mit der reflektierenden Wandinstallation aus glänzendem Metall.

New Seaside Interiors   Barbara Becker

Right: The master bathroom is wrapped in white Bisazza mosaic tiles. Both the mirror and chair were designed by Cedri/Martini.
Below: A Venini chandelier hangs above the custom bed, clad in fake leather.

À droite : La salle de bains principale est tapissée de carreaux de mosaïque blancs de Bisazza. Le miroir et la chaise sont de Cedri/Martini.
En bas : Un lustre de Venini au-dessus du lit réalisé sur mesure et recouvert de skaï.

Rechts: Das Hauptbadezimmer ist mit weißen Bisazza-Mosaikfliesen ausgekleidet. Sowohl der Spiegel als auch der Stuhl wurden von Cedri/Martini entworfen.
Unten: Ein Venini-Kronleuchter hängt über dem maßgefertigten, mit Kunstleder verkleideten Bett.

Above: "Space Panel" lights from Superieur are arranged above a sofa from Meridiani. The "Rasta" poufs were created by Paulo Haubert for Avec.
Right: In one corner of the master bedroom, a music stand attests to Becker's talent as a violin player. The armchair in the foreground is Hans Wegner's famous "Flag Halyard Chair".
Facing page: An antique African bed has been transformed into a coffee table in the living room. Eero Aarnio's "Bubble Chair" hangs from the ceiling.

En haut : Des luminaires « Space Panel » de chez Supérieur sont alignés au-dessus d'un canapé de chez Meridiani. Les poufs « Rasta » ont été créés par Paulo Haubert pour Avec.
À droite : Dans un coin de la chambre principale, le pupitre devant lequel Becker s'installe pour jouer du violon. Au premier plan, le célèbre fauteuil « Flag Halyard Chair » de Hans Wegner.
Page de droite : Dans le séjour, un ancien lit africain reconverti en table basse et une « Bubble Chair » d'Eero Aarnio.

Oben: „Space Panel"-Leuchtkörper von Superieur sind über einem Sofa von Meridiani installiert. Die „Rasta"-Puffs wurden von Paulo Haubert für Avec geschaffen.
Rechts: In einer Ecke des Hauptschlafzimmers zeugt ein Notenständer von Barbaras Talent zum Geigenspiel. Der Lehnstuhl im Vordergrund ist Hans Wegners berühmter „Flag Halyard Chair".
Gegenüberliegende Seite: Ein antikes afrikanisches Bett ist im Wohnzimmer in einen Sofatisch verwandelt worden. Eero Aarnios „Bubble Chair" hängt von der Decke herab.

New Seaside Interiors   Barbara Becker

Marbrisa
Acapulco, Mexico

Haut perchée au-dessus de la baie d'Acapulco, Marbrisa, de l'architecte John Lautner, est vertigineuse, spectaculaire et originale. Pour Frank Escher, spécialiste de Lautner : « Ce qui est superbe, c'est qu'on dirait une extension de la topographie. » Le niveau supérieur saille de la pente escarpée. Plus bas, des rochers ont été intégrés pour servir de murs aux chambres. Achevée en 1973, la maison fut conçue comme une retraite pour les week-ends. Le niveau supérieur devait être protégé par des baies vitrées mais, compte tenu de la douceur du climat, le propriétaire a décidé de le laisser ouvert aux éléments. Lautner l'a ceint de douves afin, selon Helena Arahuete qui l'a assisté, « de donner une impression d'eau s'écoulant dans la baie en contrebas ». Les formes fluides de la plateforme cachent la vue de certains bâtiments, le concept étant de « créer un espace ouvert et infini ».

Perched high above Acapulco Bay, architect John Lautner's Marbrisa is vertiginous, dramatic and original. For Lautner expert Frank Escher, "what is so beautiful is that it feels like an extension of the topography". The upper level is cantilevered out from the steep slope. Below, boulders thrust inside to become bedroom walls. Completed in 1973, the house was conceived as a weekend retreat. The initial intent was to enclose the upper living deck with glass. The client, however, decided the climate was so mild that it should be left open. Instead, Lautner ringed it with a moat. "He wanted to create the feeling of water flowing into the bay below," recalls Helena Arahuete, who assisted on the project. The free-flowing platform, meanwhile, was devised to block out views of certain buildings. "The concept," she adds, "was to create a feeling of unlimited, open space."

Hoch über der Bucht von Acapulco erhebt sich schwindelerregend, dramatisch und in überwältigender Originalität das Bauwerk Marbrisa des Architekten John Lautner. Für den Lautner-Experten Frank Escher ist „das Schöne daran, dass man es ... als Erweiterung der Landschaft empfindet". Die obere Ebene ist in den steilen Abhang hineingeschnitten. Unterhalb wurde Felsgestein zur Bildung der Schlafzimmerwände in das Innere einbezogen. Das 1973 vollendete Haus war als Feriendomizil geplant. Ursprünglich sollte der obere Wohnbereich verglast werden. Der Auftraggeber beschloss jedoch, ihn angesichts des milden Klimas offen zu lassen. Lautner umgab ihn daraufhin stattdessen mit einem Wasserlauf. „Er wollte ... den Eindruck von in die Bucht hinabfließendem Wasser hervorrufen", erinnert sich Helena Arahuete, die Lautner bei dem Projekt assistierte. Die frei schwebende Anlage der Plattform sollte den Blick auf bestimmte Gebäude verstellen. „Das Konzept war, ein Gefühl grenzenloser Weite heraufzubeschwören."

Below: Murals were added to the walls of the master bedroom at a later date.
Facing page: Mexican artist Antonio Farreny created a number of built-in elements for the house. Among them, this geometric metal sideboard.

En bas : Les peintures murales de la chambre des maîtres ont été réalisées plus tardivement.
Page de droite : L'artiste mexicain Antonio Farreny a créé plusieurs éléments encastrés pour la maison, dont cette console géométrique en métal.

Unten: Zu einem späteren Zeitpunkt wurden im Hauptschlafzimmer Wandmalereien angebracht.
Gegenüberliegende Seite: Der mexikanische Künstler Antonio Farreny schuf für das Haus eine Reihe von Einbau-Elementen, darunter das Sideboard aus Metall mit geometrischen Einlagen.

Previous pages: The upper level is home to an open concrete living terrace, surrounded by a 1.80-metre-wide moat, in which you can swim. The platform is accessed from the entrance by a curvaceous bridge.
Above: The steel entry gate was designed by artist Mathias Goeritz, who is best known for his work with Luis Barragán on the Torres Satélite in Mexico City.

Pages précédentes : Le niveau supérieur accueille une terrasse en béton servant de séjour ouvert aux éléments et entourée d'une douve de 1,80 m de large dans laquelle on peut nager. On y accède depuis l'entrée par une passerelle aux lignes ondoyantes.
En haut : Le portail en acier de l'entrée est une œuvre de l'artiste Mathias Goeritz, surtout connu pour son travail avec Luis Barragán sur les Torres Satélite à Mexico.

Vorhergehende Seiten: Die obere Ebene nimmt eine offene Wohnterrasse ein, umgeben von einem 1,80 Meter breiten Wasserlauf, in dem man sogar schwimmen kann. Zu dieser Ebene gelangt man vom Eingang her über eine geschwungene Brücke.
Oben: Das stählerne Eingangstor ist ein Entwurf des Künstlers Mathias Goeritz, der durch seine Zusammenarbeit mit Luis Barragán an den „Torres Satélite" in Mexico City bekannt wurde.

Below: A painting by Jordi Boldó hangs above a copper cabinet created by interior designer Arthur Elrod, for whom Lautner built another famous house, in Palm Springs.

En bas : Une toile de Jordi Boldó au-dessus d'un meuble en cuivre créé par le décorateur Arthur Elrod, pour qui Lautner a construit une autre maison célèbre à Palm Springs.

Unten: Ein Gemälde von Jordi Boldó hängt über einem Sideboard aus Kupfer nach einem Design von Arthur Elrod. Für den Innenarchitekten und Designer Elrod entwarf Lautner ein nicht weniger berühmtes Haus in Palm Springs.

Facing page: The five bedrooms on the lower level are glazed. Here, the master bedroom, with its recessed tub and two Pierre Paulin "Ribbon" armchairs.
Above: A steel sculpture by artist Eduardo Wegman.

Page de gauche : Les cinq chambres de l'étage inférieur sont protégées de vitres. Ici, la chambre des maîtres, avec sa baignoire encastrée et deux fauteuils « Ribbon » de Pierre Paulin.
En haut : Une sculpture en acier d'Eduardo Wegman.

Gegenüberliegende Seite: Die fünf Schlafzimmer in der unteren Etage sind verglast. Hier das Hauptschlafzimmer mit seiner in den Boden eingelassenen Wanne und zwei „Ribbon Chairs" von Pierre Paulin.
Oben: Eine Stahlskulptur des Künstlers Eduardo Wegman.

Mima & César Reyes

Naguabo, Puerto Rico

Après avoir acheté un terrain sur la côte est de Puerto Rico, le psychiatre César Reyes et sa femme Mima ont contacté l'artiste Jorge Pardo. Au lieu de commander un tableau, ils lui ont demandé de leur construire une maison. Pardo fut très inspiré par la beauté « ravageuse » du site. « Il est spectaculaire, escarpé. Le défi consistait à y faire entrer le plus de ciel et de mer possible tout en préservant l'intimité des occupants. » Délaissant le verre, il a opté pour une structure en béton ouverte ceinte d'écrans métalliques ouvragés. « Il pleut à l'intérieur », admet-il, « mais ça sèche vite. On est sous les tropiques. » Parmi les autres détails saisissants : une piscine rouge sang et le carrelage aux couleurs changeantes. Il passe du jaune sur le devant de la maison au bleu à l'arrière.

When psychiatrist César Reyes and his wife Mima bought a plot of land on Puerto Rico's east coast, they decided to commission a work from artist Jorge Pardo. Instead of asking him to create a painting, they requested that he build a house. Pardo was greatly inspired by the "devastatingly beautiful" location. "It's a very dramatic, tight site," he says. "The challenge was to get as much sky and sea as possible... and yet maintain a maximum of privacy." He decided not to use any glass. Instead, he left the concrete structure open and wrapped it in ornate metal screens. "It gets wet inside," he admits, "but it also dries quickly. That's how it is in the tropics." Other striking features include the blood-red swimming pool and the constantly shifting colour of the floor tiles. They start off yellow at the front of the house and end up blue at the back.

Als der Psychiater César Reyes und seine Frau Mima ein Grundstück an der Ostküste von Puerto Rico kauften, beschlossen sie, den Künstler Jorge Pardo statt mit einem Gemälde mit dem Bau eines Hauses zu beauftragen. Pardo war stark inspiriert von der „überwältigend schönen" Lage. „Es handelt sich um eine sehr dramatische, in sich geschlossene Aussicht", sagt er. „Die Herausforderung bestand darin, so viel Himmel und Meer wie möglich einzubeziehen ... und dennoch ein Maximum an Abgeschiedenheit zu bewahren." Er beschloss, keinerlei Glas zu verwenden. Stattdessen legte er die Betonstruktur offen an und umgab sie mit dekorativ verzierten Metallgittern. „Innen wird es nass", gibt er zu, „aber es trocknet auch schnell wieder. So ist es eben in den Tropen." Weitere verblüffende Hingucker sind der blutrote Swimmingpool und die ständig abwechselnden Farben der Fußbodenfliesen. An der Vorderseite des Hauses setzen sie mit Gelb ein, an der Rückseite enden sie in Blau.

Previous pages: *The kitchen units were custom-made from laminated cedar wood. The rocking chairs are by Charles and Ray Eames.*
Facing page: *The large artwork, entitled "Hola Carola", was created by Pardo in homage to the owner's daughter.*
Above: *The grillwork was custom-made from tubes of steel.*
Right: *A George Nelson "Bubble" lamp hangs above a four-poster in the master bedroom.*
Following pages: *An Eames "Lounge Chair and Ottoman" on a deck outside; vintage Mexican folk masks and Elizabeth Peyton portraits of Liam Gallagher and Kurt Cobain.*

Pages précédentes : *Les éléments de cuisine sont en cèdre laminé et les rocking-chairs de Charles et Ray Eames.*
Page de gauche : *La grande toile, intitulée « Hola Carola », est un hommage de Pardo à la fille des maîtres de maison.*
En haut : *La grille a été réalisée avec des tubes d'acier.*
À droite : *Dans la chambre des maîtres, un lit à baldaquin.*
Pages suivantes : *Une chaise longue avec repose-pied de Eames sur une terrasse. Des masques mexicains anciens et des portraits de Liam Gallagher et de Kurt Cobain signés Elizabeth Peyton.*

Vorhergehende Seiten: *Die Küchenmöbel sind maßgefertigt aus laminiertem Zedernholz. Die Schaukelstühle sind von Charles und Ray Eames.*
Gegenüberliegende Seite: *Das große Gemälde mit dem Titel „Hola Carola" ist eine Hommage Pardos an die Tochter der Besitzer.*
Oben: *Das Gitterwerk wurde aus Stahlrohren maßgefertigt.*
Rechts: *Eine „Bubble"-Lampe von George Nelson über dem Pfostenbett.*
Folgende Seiten: *Ein „Lounge Chair" und „Ottomane" von Eames auf einer Terrasse. Landestypische Masken und von Elizabeth Peyton gemalte Porträts von Liam Gallagher und Kurt Cobain.*

Rudolf Nureyev
Saint Barths, French West Indies

À la fin de sa vie, Rudolf Noureev possédait sept propriétés dont une maison perchée sur des rochers sur la côte est de Saint Barths, construite en 1962 pour un amiral. Aujourd'hui, elle appartient à une Française, Jeanne Audy-Rowland, qui l'entretient en hommage à la grande étoile du ballet. Elle a inscrit certaines de ses citations sur les murs et construit une datcha mais, le plus frappant, c'est l'immense terrasse en teck sur laquelle Noureev dansait. Il avait également fait creuser une plateforme dans la roche sur laquelle il aimait dormir. En dehors des visites de Jackie Kennedy deux ou trois fois par an, il y menait une vie solitaire. « Très sobre, presque ascétique », se souvient Audy-Rowland. Elle a beau achever la décoration qu'il n'a pas terminé, elle croît fermement : « Ça reste sa maison, pas la mienne. »

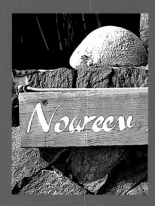

At the end of his life, dancer Rudolf Nureyev owned seven properties. One was a house perched on rocks on the eastern coast of Saint Barths, originally built for an American admiral in 1962. Today, it is owned by a Frenchwoman called Jeanne Audy-Rowland, who maintains it as an homage to the late star's memory. She has inscribed some of his quotes on the walls and built a datcha. The main feature, however, remains the huge teak deck, on which Nureyev used to dance. He also carved a platform into the rock, where he would often sleep. Jackie Kennedy would visit two or three times a year, but otherwise he remained quite solitary. "He lived very soberly," remarks Audy-Rowland. "Almost like an ascetic." He never really finished off the decoration. Audy-Rowland may have done that, but still firmly believes: "It's his house, not mine."

Am Ende seines Lebens nannte der Tänzer Rudolf Nurejew sieben Anwesen sein Eigen. Eines davon war ein auf Fels gebautes Haus an der Ostküste von St. Barths, das im Jahr 1962 ursprünglich für einen amerikanischen Admiral errichtet worden war. Heute ist dessen Besitzerin eine Französin namens Jeanne Audy-Rowland, die es als Hommage an den verstorbenen Künstler erhält. Sie hat Zitate Nurejews an die Wänden geschrieben und eine Datscha gebaut. Der Hauptakzent ist und bleibt jedoch die große Plattform aus Teakholz, auf der Nurejew zu tanzen pflegte. Er schnitt auch ein flaches Plateau in den Felsen, wo er häufig schlief. Jackie Kennedy besuchte ihn ein- oder zweimal im Jahr – eine der seltenen Besucherinnen bzw. Besucher, denn er wohnte recht zurückgezogen. „Er lebte sehr solide", bemerkt Jeanne Audy-Rowland. „Fast wie ein Asket." Es gelang ihm aber nicht, die Einrichtung zu vollenden. Jeanne Audy-Rowland hätte es tun können, aber sie ist der Überzeugung: „Es ist sein Haus, nicht meines."

Previous pages and above: A teak sofa and Balinese loungers on the deck, which Nureyev built to dance on. Guests would sit on the stairs to watch his performances.
Right: The small seawater pool was constructed by current owner, Jeanne Audy-Rowland.

Pages précédentes et ci-dessus : Un canapé en teck et des chaises longues balinaises sur la terrasse, construite par Noureev pour y danser. Les invités s'asseyaient sur les marches pour le regarder.
À droite : La petite piscine d'eau de mer a été construite par la propriétaire actuelle, Jeanne Audy-Rowland.

Vorhergehende Seiten und oben: Ein Teakholz-Sofa und Liegestühle aus Bali auf der von Nurejew gebauten Tanz-Plattform. Die Gäste saßen auf den Stufen, um ihm zuzuschauen.
Rechts: Der kleine Pool mit Meerwasser wurde von der jetzigen Besitzerin, Jeanne Audy-Rowland, angelegt.

Right: *The two rustic Balinese chairs in front of the bedroom of Audy-Rowland's son Nicolas are about 100 years old.*
Below: *The kitchen counter originally belonged to an English haberdashery.*

À droite : *Les deux sièges rustiques balinais devant la chambre de Nicolas, le fils d'Audy-Rowland, sont presque centenaires.*
En bas : *Le comptoir de la cuisine provient d'une vieille mercerie anglaise.*

Rechts: *Die beiden rustikalen balinesischen Stühle vor dem Schlafzimmer von Audy-Rowlands Sohn Nicolas sind etwa 100 Jahre alt.*
Unten: *Die Küchentheke gehörte ursprünglich zur Einrichtung einer englischen Kurzwarenhandlung.*

Facing page: The house offers complete privacy and 180° views of
the sea.
Above: Nureyev's piano still stands in the library. The coffee table is
17th-century Spanish.
Right: In Nicolas' bedroom is a collage of images of the dancer.

Page de gauche : Jouissant d'une intimité totale, la maison offre une
vue à 180° sur la mer.
En haut : La bibliothèque abrite toujours le piano de Noureev. La
table basse espagnole date du XVIIᵉ siècle.
À droite : Dans la chambre de Nicolas, un collage d'images du
danseur.

Gegenüberliegende Seite: Das Haus bietet vollständige Abgeschie-
denheit und 180-Grad-Ausblicke aufs Meer.
Oben: Nurejews Klavier steht noch in der Bibliothek. Der spanische
Tisch stammt aus dem 17. Jahrhundert.
Rechts: Im Schlafzimmer von Nicolas befindet sich eine Collage mit
Bildnissen des Tänzers.

Daan Nelemans
Manzanillo, Costa Rica

Adolescent, Daan Nelemans rêvait d'habiter sur une île déserte. « Je m'imaginais vivant loin du stress du monde. » Ce Hollandais n'a pas encore trouvé son île mais sa propriété de six hectares est certainement sauvage : elle est située au cœur d'une jungle sur la côte caribéenne du Costa Rica, à 200 m d'une plage de sable blanc. Il l'a plantée d'arbres fruitiers et de fleurs tropicales. Outre la sienne, il a construit quatre autres maisons qu'il loue aux touristes, dont un « rancho indien » avec un toit en feuilles de palmier et des murs en écorce. Sa propre maison est également aménagée à la mode primitive. D'Amsterdam, il n'a apporté que deux platines et a construit tout le reste lui-même. « Je suis assez bricoleur », explique-t-il. « Pas le genre à rester dans mon hamac. »

When Daan Nelemans was a teenager, his dream was to live on a tropical island. "I thought I'd like to live away from the stress of the world," he recalls. He never quite made it to an island, but the setting of his house is certainly quite tropical. At the heart of the jungle on the Caribbean coast of Costa Rica, it is just 200 metres from a white, sandy beach. On his six-hectare property, the Dutchman has planted tropical flowers and fruit trees. He has also built four other houses, which he rents out to visitors. Among them, an "Indian Rancho", which has palm leaves on the roof and bark on the walls. The furnishings in Nelemans's own house are just as primitive. From Amsterdam, he brought a pair of turntables, but made almost everything else himself. "I'm a person who likes to do things," he asserts. "I'm not just going to lie down in a hammock!"

Als Teenager pflegte Daan Nelemans von einer tropischen Insel zu träumen. „Ich bildete mir damals ein, fern vom Stress der Welt leben zu wollen", erinnert er sich. Zu einer Insel hat es zwar nicht gereicht, aber zur tropischen Umgebung durchaus. Sein Haus liegt im Herzen des Dschungels an der Karibischen Küste von Costa Rica, nur 200 Meter von einem weißen Sandstrand entfernt. Auf seinem sechs Hektar großen Grundstück hat der Niederländer tropische Blumen und Früchte gepflanzt. Auch hat er vier weitere Häuser errichtet, die er an Besucher vermietet, darunter eine palmblattgedeckte „Indianerhütte" („Indian Rancho") mit Rinde an den Wänden. Die Einrichtung von Nelemans eigenem Haus ist ebenso primitiv. Aus Amsterdam brachte er zwei Plattenspieler mit, doch fast alles andere hat er selbst gebaut. „Ich bin ein Mensch, der gern aktiv ist", meint er. „Ich mag etwas tun, nicht nur in der Hängematte liegen."

Left: Camp-style cooking in the kitchen.
Below: A cow's skull adorns the front of a piece of furniture, which houses two turntables brought from the Netherlands.
Following pages: Shells and a papaya sit on a locally built coffee table. The hammock is made from cotton.

À gauche : La cuisine ouverte aux éléments.
En bas : Un crâne de vache orne un meuble qui abrite deux platines rapportées de Hollande.
Double page suivante : Des coquillages et une papaye sur une table basse de la région. Le hamac est en coton.

Links: In der Küche wird im Camper-Stil gekocht.
Unten: Ein Rinderschädel schmückt ein Möbelstück, das zwei Plattenspieler aus den Niederlanden in sich birgt.
Folgende Seiten: Muscheln und eine Papaya liegen auf einem Sofatisch einheimischer Produktion. Die Hängematte ist aus Baumwolle.

Previous pages: At the heart of the jungle, Nelemans's property is just 200 metres from the Caribbean Sea. The structure with the sloped roof is a rental property called the "Indian Rancho". The vintage car was shipped from the Netherlands. His own house centres around an impressive spiral staircase made from catcha wood.
Facing page: The seating area in Nelemans's own house. The wooden chairs were bought locally and the ceiling light made from a calabash and debris found on the beach.

Pages précédentes : Située au cœur de la jungle, la propriété de Nelemans n'est qu'à 200 m de la mer des Caraïbes. La hutte au toit pentu, le « rancho indien », est à louer. La vieille automobile a été apportée de Hollande. Sa propre maison est bâtie autour d'un bel escalier en colimaçon réalisé en catcha.
Page de gauche : Le coin salon de la maison de Nelemans. Les fauteuils en bois ont été achetés dans la région. Le lustre a été réalisé avec une calebasse et des débris trouvés sur la plage.

Vorhergehende Seiten: Obwohl mitten im Dschungel, liegt das Besitztum von Daan Nelemans nur 200 Meter von der Karibischen See entfernt. Das Häuschen mit dem steilen Spitzdach ist die sogenannte Indianerhütte („Indian Rancho"). Der Oldtimer wurde aus den Niederlanden importiert. Sein eigenes Haus hat eine eindrucksvolle Wendeltreppe aus Catchaholz zum Mittelpunkt.
Gegenüberliegende Seite: Der Sitzbereich in Nelemans' Haus. Die hölzernen Stühle stammen aus lokaler Produktion, und die Deckenleuchte entstand aus einer Kalabasse und Strandgut.

White Wonder
Iporanga, Brazil

L'élégantissime plage d'Iporanga se trouve à 90 minutes au nord de São Paolo, au cœur d'un parc naturel. Comme le dit l'architecte Isay Weinfeld « Ici, on ne peut pas se permettre d'habiter dans une simple cabane. » Il a donc bâti une maison sur deux niveaux, constituée de deux structures rectangulaires posées l'une sur l'autre. Celle du haut est équipée de moucharabiehs en aluminium peint, une référence aux origines moyen-orientales du maître de maison. Partout, le décor est « très zen, très calme et très blanc ». Pour ajouter un peu de texture, Weinfeld a lambrissé le mur du fond du séjour ouvert de planches en peroba récupérées dans une ferme du XVIIIᵉ siècle. Dehors, d'un bout de la piscine, il a créé un coin salon sous toile, dont le sol est recouvert de sable. « C'est comme une extension de la plage », expliquent les propriétaires.

Iporanga beach is located some 90 minutes to the north of São Paulo. Situated at the heart of a nature reserve, it is decidedly chic. As architect Isay Weinfeld says: "It's not the right place just to design a simple cottage." Instead, he built a two-storey house, which consists of a pair of box-like structures, placed one on top of the other. The upper one is clad in a *moucharabieh* screen made from painted aluminium: a reference to the Middle Eastern origins of the man of the house. Throughout, the ambience is "very zen, very quiet" and very white. To add some texture, Weinfeld clad the back wall of the open-plan living space with reclaimed peroba wood from an 18th-century farm. Outside, at one end of the pool, he created a tent-like living area, whose floor is covered in sand. As the owners say: "It's almost like an extension of the beach."

Nördlich von São Paulo und von dort in etwa 90 Minuten zu erreichen, erstreckt sich der Strand von Iporanga. Er liegt im Herzen eines Naturreservats und ist entschieden schick. Wie der Architekt Isay Weinfeld sagt: „Dies ist nicht der Ort, ein einfaches Cottage zu entwerfen." Stattdessen errichtete er ein zweigeschossiges Haus aus zwei aufeinanderruhenden schachtelförmigen Kuben. Der obere Kubus ist mit einer Moucharabieh, einem filigranen Gitterwerk aus bemaltem Aluminium verkleidet – eine Anspielung auf das Herkunftsland des Hausherrn im Mittleren Osten. Die Ausstrahlung des Bauwerks ist insgesamt „sehr ruhig, sehr Zen-meditativ" und sehr weiß. Um etwas Textur hinzuzufügen, verkleidete Weinfeld die Rückwand des offenen Wohnbereichs mit restauriertem Perobaholz einer Abbruchfarm aus dem 18. Jahrhundert. Im Freien schuf er an einem Ende des Pools einen zeltähnlichen Wohnbereich mit sandbedecktem Boden. Er ist nach Meinung der Besitzer „fast wie ein erweiterter Strand".

Previous pages: An outdoor, steel-framed sitting area is located at the end of the pool. The chair is the "Diz" model by Brazilian designer Sergio Rodrigues.
Above: "Sillon" chairs by Argentinian designer Laura O. are grouped around a Grete Jalk coffee table in the main living area.
Right: Weinfeld designed ipé wood coffee tables for the outdoor lounge area. A stretched Sunbrella canvas provides welcome shade.

Pages précédentes : Un coin salon extérieur sous une structure en aluminium borde la piscine. Le fauteuil « Diz » est du designer brésilien Sergio Rodrigues.
En haut : Dans le séjour principal, des fauteuils « Sillon » de la designer argentine Laura O. sont regroupés autour d'une table basse de Grete Jalk.
À droite : Weinfeld a dessiné les tables basses en ipé pour le coin salon extérieur. Un auvent en toile Sunbrella offre une ombre bienvenue.

Vorhergehende Seiten: Stahlgerahmter Sitzbereich am Ende des Pools. Der Stuhl ist das „Diz"-Modell des brasilianischen Designers Sergio Rodrigues.
Oben: „Sillon"-Stühle der argentinischen Designerin Laura O. sind im zentralen Wohnbereich um einen Beistelltisch von Grete Jalk gruppiert.
Rechts: Weinfeld entwarf die Beistelltischchen aus Ipé-Holz für den Außenbereich. Ein darüber gespanntes Zeltdach liefert willkommenen Schatten.

Right: The bed in the son's room was designed by Laura O.
Below: Photos by Michael Wesely hang above Laura O.'s "Cubo Cuadrado" banquette in the family room.

À droite : Le lit de la chambre du fils a été dessiné par Laura O.
En bas : Dans le salon familial, des photos de Michael Wesely sont accrochées au-dessus d'une banquette « Cubo Cuadrado » de Laura O.

Rechts: Das Bett im Zimmer des Sohnes wurde von Laura O. entworfen.
Unten: Fotos von Michael Wesely hängen über Laura O.'s „Cubo Cuadrado"-Liege im Familienzimmer.

Previous pages: The house is deliberately open to provide constant views of the surrounding nature. The top floor is encased in a painted aluminium "moucharabieh".
Right: A view into the master bedroom.
Below: A metal fireplace is set into a wall made from reclaimed peroba wood. A cowhide covers a banquette, which acts as a coffee table.

Double page précédente : La maison a été conçue pour s'ouvrir sur la nature environnante. L'étage est protégé par des moucharabiehs en aluminium peint.
À droite : La chambre principale.
En bas : Une cheminée en métal encastrée dans un mur lambrissé en planches de peroba recyclées. Une peau de vache est jetée sur une banquette faisant office de table basse.

Vorhergehende Seiten: Das Haus ist bewusst offen angelegt, um einen ungehinderten Blick auf die Natur zu gewähren. Die obere Etage wurde mit einem filigranen Gitterwerk aus bemaltem Aluminium im maurischen Stil eingefasst.
Rechts: Ein Blick in das Hauptschlafzimmer.
Unten: Auf eine Wand aus restauriertem alten Perobaholz wurde der Metall-Kamin gesetzt. Ein Kuhfell liegt auf einer als Sofatisch dienenden Sitzbank.

Above: A sofa and chairs by Laura O. ring a dining table, which Weinfeld designed from a local wood called freijo. The "Bubble" lamps are by George Nelson.
Right: A pair of "Bombo" stools by Stefano Giovannoni in the custom-built kitchen.

En haut : Un canapé et des fauteuils de Laura O. autour d'une table créée par Weinfeld dans un bois local, le freijo. Les lampes « Bubble » sont de George Nelson.
À droite : Dans la cuisine construite sur mesure, une paire de tabourets « Bombo » de Stefano Giovannoni.

Oben: Ein Sofa und Sessel von Laura O. um einen Esstisch, den Weinfeld aus einheimischem Freijo-Holz schuf. Die „Bubble"-Lampen darüber sind von George Nelson.
Rechts: Zwei „Bombo"-Hocker von Stefano Giovannoni in der maß-gefertigten Küche.

Azul García Uriburu

Faro José Ignacio, Uruguay

Pour l'architecte argentine Azul García Uriburu, le minuscule village de pêcheurs de Faro José Ignacio est une affaire de famille. Sa mère y dirige une guest-house et son père Nicolás (un artiste célèbre) vit non loin. Son mari Marcos Pereda et elle y passent leurs vacances avec leurs quatre enfants, appréciant la plage tranquille, les phoques, les dauphins et le fait de pouvoir se rendre à pied n'importe où. La maison qu'elle a construite sur la plage venteuse est symétrique et conçue pour s'intégrer dans le paysage. La façade est tapissée de bardeaux en pin et les intérieurs sont peints couleur sable. « C'est très monochrome », explique-t-elle. « Ce sont les gens qui apportent de la couleur. » Quant au fait de vivre au bord de la mer : « C'est merveilleux. Ici, on a vraiment l'impression d'être seuls sur terre. »

For Argentine architect Azul García Uriburu, the tiny fishing village of Faro José Ignacio is all about the family. Her father, Nicolás (a famous artist), lives nearby and her mother runs a local guesthouse. She and her husband, Marcos Pereda, own a house directly on the windswept beach, where they spend holidays with their four children. Ask García Uriburu why she likes the locality and she'll mention the safe beach, the seals and dolphins in the sea, and the fact that you can walk everywhere. She designed the symmetrical house herself, with the goal of integrating it into the natural setting. The façade is clad with pine and the interiors painted a sand colour. "It's very monochromatic," she says. "It's people who add colour." And how's life on the beach? "It's incredible," she admits. "When we're there, we feel that we really are alone on Earth."

Für die argentinische Architektin Azul García Uriburu ist das winzige Fischerdorf Faro José Ignacio ein wichtiger Dreh- und Angelpunkt ihres Familienlebens. Ihr Vater Nicolás (ein berühmter Künstler) lebt ganz in der Nähe, ihre Mutter führt am Ort ein Gästehaus, und Azul sowie Ehemann Marcos Pereda besitzen unmittelbar am windgepeitschten Strand ein Haus, wo sie mit ihren vier Kindern die Ferien verbringen. Sobald man Azul García Uriburu fragt, warum sie den Ort mag, wird sie den sicheren Strand, die Seehunde und Delphine im Meer anführen sowie die Tatsache, dass man überallhin zu Fuß gehen kann. Sie selbst hat das symmetrische Haus mit der Absicht entworfen, dass es sich harmonisch in die natürliche Umgebung integriert. Die Fassade ist mit Kiefernholz verkleidet, die Innenwände wurden sandfarben gestrichen. „Es ist alles sehr monochrom", räumt sie ein, „es sind die Menschen, die Farbe hinzufügen." Und sie sagt: „Es ist unglaublich, wenn wir uns hier aufhalten, haben wir das Gefühl, allein auf der Erde zu sein."

Previous page: Son Marcial and youngest daughter Esperanza fool around on the dunes.
Above: The house is a study in symmetry. There are terraces both front and back, in the center is the living room.
Right: Daughters Azul (left) and Milagros with the family cats.
Facing page: The table on the back terrace is used for tea and dinner. All the furniture was designed by Isabelle Firmin Didot.
Following pages: Inside, the ceiling is made from reeds and eucalyptus beams, and the fireplaces from local stone.

Page précédente : Marcial, le fils, et Esperanza, la benjamine, jouent dans les dunes.
En haut : La structure est parfaitement symétrique, avec des terrasses à l'avant et à l'arrière et, au centre, un séjour.
À droite : Les filles Azul et Milagros câlinant les chats de la maison.
Page de droite : Les meubles sur la terrasse à l'arrière de la maison ont été créés par Isabelle Firmin Didot.
Pages suivantes : L'intérieur privilégie les matériaux naturels. Le plafond est en roseaux et poutres d'eucalyptus, les cheminées en pierres locales et les sols recouverts de tapis en crin végétal.

Vorhergehende Seite: Sohn Marcial und die jüngste Tochter Esperanza tollen in den Dünen herum.
Oben: Das Haus ist eine Studie der Symmetrie. Terrassen erstrecken sich an Vorder- wie Rückseite. In der Mitte befindet sich das Wohnzimmer.
Rechts: Die Töchter Azul und Milagros mit den Katzen der Familie.
Gegenüberliegende Seite: Alle Möbel auf der hinteren Terrasse wurden von Isabelle Firmin Didot entworfen.
Folgende Seiten: Die Decke im Inneren des Hauses besteht aus Eukalyptusholzbalken und Schilfgras. Der Kamin ist aus einheimischen Steinen, und die Böden sind mit Seegrasmatten bedeckt.

New Seaside Interiors   Azul García Uriburu

Michel Grether

Punta del Este, Uruguay

Selon l'architecte Michel Grether, Punta Ballena est le seul endroit sur la côte Atlantique d'Amérique du Sud où l'on voit le soleil se coucher. Il est indéniable que la maison qu'il a construite lui-même sur une falaise jouit d'une vue imprenable. Pour creuser la roche, il a loué un marteau-piqueur et acheté des explosifs. Il a dessiné le mobilier rustique, la robinetterie et les lampes. Dans l'une des deux chambres, un affleurement de roche sert de tête de lit ; dans une autre, une simple gouttière a été creusée pour chasser l'eau de pluie. L'objectif était de créer la parfaite demeure écologique. Avec les pierres extraites, Grether a créé des murs et des colonnes, puis couvert la structure de végétation. « La maison est camouflée, on ne la voit que de la mer », déclare-t-il. Parapentiste chevronné, le toit lui sert également de piste de décollage et d'atterrissage.

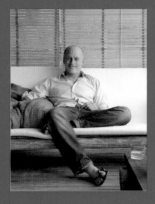

According to architect Michel Grether, Punta Ballena is the only spot on South America's Atlantic coast where you can see the sun set. He certainly has one of the best views of it from the clifftop house, which he built himself. He hired a pneumatic drill and bought explosives to hollow out the rock. He constructed the rustic furniture and even designed the taps and lamps. In one of the two bedrooms, an exposed rock face acts as a headboard. In the guest bathroom, another is fitted with a simple gutter to drain away rainwater, which infiltrates the house. Grether's goal was to create a perfectly ecological dwelling. He reused excavated rocks for walls and columns, and covered the structure in vegetation. "The house is camouflaged," he asserts. "You can only see it from the sea." The roof also has another use – a take-off and landing strip for his passion: hang-gliding.

Nach Meinung des Architekten Michel Grether ist Punta Ballena der einzige Ort an der südamerikanischen Atlantikküste, von dem aus man einen richtigen Sonnenuntergang erleben kann. Den besten Blick erlaubt ihm mit Sicherheit sein Haus auf den Felsen, das er selbst erbaut hat. Mit einem geliehenen Presslufthammer und Sprengmunition höhlte er eigenhändig den Felsen aus. Er fertigte die rustikalen Möbel und entwarf sogar die Wasserhähne und Lampen. In einem der beiden Schlafzimmer dient ein freigelegter Stein sozusagen als Kopfende. Ein anderer im Gästebad weist einen Ablauf für das ins Haus dringende Regenwasser auf. Grethers Ziel war ein vollkommen ökologisches Bauwerk. Er nutzte gesprengte, übrig gebliebene Felsbrocken zum Bau von Wänden und Säulen und überdeckte die gesamte Struktur mit Vegetation. „Das Haus ist getarnt", stellt er fest, „man kann es nur vom Meer aus sehen." Das Dach wird doppelt genutzt, denn es dient auch als Start- und Landeplatz für seine Leidenschaft: das Drachenfliegen.

Previous pages: Excavated rocks were used for the columns inside the house. The chairs and sofa on the outdoor seating area were made by Grether from pine and eucalyptus logs. Fabrics created by north Argentinian Indians are draped over two stools in front of the kitchen.
Above: Above the Grether-made sofa is a fish caught in Acapulco in 1967 by a friend's grandfather. The striped fabric was brought back from Turkey. The stove originally belonged to an English country house.
Right: The kitchen walls were decorated by an artist friend, Hugo Arias.

Pages précédentes : Les pierres extraites ont servi à créer des colonnes dans la maison. Les fauteuils et le canapé de la terrasse ont été réalisés par Grether dans du sapin et de l'eucalyptus abattus sur sa propriété. Devant la cuisine, deux tabourets recouverts d'étoffes tissées par les Indiens du nord de l'Argentine.
En haut : Au-dessus du canapé, un espadon pêché à Acapulco en 1967 par le grand-père d'un ami. Le tissu rayé a été rapporté de Turquie. Le poêle provient d'une maison de campagne anglaise.
À droite : Les murs de la cuisine ont été décorés par un ami artiste, Hugo Arias.

Vorhergehende Seiten: Gesprengte Gesteinsbrocken dienten zum Bau der Säulen im Haus. Die Sessel und die Sitzbank im Außenbereich wurden von Grether aus gefällten Pinien und Eukalyptusbäumen des Grundstücks gefertigt. Webdecken nordargentinischer Indianer sind über zwei Hocker vor der Küche drapiert.
Oben: Über dem Sofa prangt ein 1967 vom Großvater eines Freundes gefangener Fisch. Der gestreifte Stoff stammt aus der Türkei, der Ofen aus einem englischen Landhaus.
Rechts: Die Wände der Küche wurden von Hugo Arias bemalt.

Right: A line of oil lamps in the entrance.
Below: Grether found the iron base of the dining table at an antique market. The top is made from eucalyptus.
Following pages: Exposed rocks are visible in the guest bedroom and bathroom. The mirror was framed with an old window, which Grether found one day while out horse riding.

À droite : Un alignement de lampes à huile dans l'entrée.
En bas : Grether a trouvé la base en fonte de sa table de salle à manger dans une foire d'antiquaires. Le plateau est en eucalyptus.
Pages suivantes : Des pierres apparentes dans la chambre d'amis et la salle de bains. Le chambranle d'une vieille fenêtre sert d'encadrement à un miroir. Grether l'a trouvé au cours d'une promenade à cheval.

Rechts: Eine Reihe Petroleumlampen im Eingangsbereich.
Unten: Grether fand die eisernen Stützen des Esstisches auf einem Antiquitätenmarkt. Die Tischplatte besteht aus Eukalyptusholz.
Folgende Seiten: Freigelegte Felsbrocken im Gästezimmer und Gästebad. Der Spiegel wurde in einen alten Fensterrahmen gefasst, ein Zufallsfund Grethers bei einem Ausritt.

Cool Classicism
Manantiales, Uruguay

L'architecte Diego Félix San Martín connaît depuis plus de vingt ans la paysagiste propriétaire de cette maison, ayant déjà construit pour elle plusieurs résidences en Argentine et collaboré avec elle sur de nombreux projets. Pour cette retraite d'été près de Punta del Este, elle a évoqué deux sources d'inspiration : la Renaissance italienne, dont l'influence est manifeste dans les nombreuses arches classiques, et les demeures traditionnelles de Marrakech, avec leurs espaces où se confondent l'intérieur et l'extérieur. L'exemple le plus frappant en est la spacieuse galerie de 12 m de long, avec un toit en jonc et verre, ouverte sur les côtés. Elle offre de merveilleuses perspectives. Comme dit San Martín : « On peut voir à travers d'un bout à l'autre de la maison. »

Architect Diego Félix San Martín has known the owner of this house for over 20 years. He has created several residences for her in Argentina and collaborated with her on numerous projects. "She's a very good landscape architect", he asserts. For this summerhouse near Punta del Este, she evoked two sources of inspiration – the Italian Renaissance and the traditional houses of Marrakech. The influence of the former can be clearly seen in the abundant use of classical arches. The latter, meanwhile, gave rise to spaces that are halfway between the indoors and outdoors. The most notable example is the 12-metre-long gallery, which is topped with a glass and cane roof, but remains open on all sides. It also offers some wonderful axial views. As San Martín says, "the best thing is that you can see all the way through the house from one side to the other".

Die Eigentümerin dieses Hauses kennt der Architekt Diego Félix San Martín seit über 20 Jahren. Er hat in Argentinien mehrere Wohnsitze für sie gebaut und mit ihr an verschiedenen Projekten zusammengearbeitet. „Sie ist eine sehr gute Landschaftsarchitektin", erklärt er. Für dieses Sommerhaus bei Punta del Este nutzte sie zwei Quellen der Inspiration – die italienische Renaissance und die traditionellen Häuser von Marrakesch. Der italienische Einfluss geht klar aus den zahlreichen klassischen Bögen hervor, während der Gedanke an Marrakesch Räume ins Leben rief, die in der Mitte zwischen drinnen und draußen angesiedelt sind. Das bemerkenswerteste Beispiel ist die zwölf Meter lange Galerie, die mit Schilfrohr und Glas gedeckt ist, aber seitlich offen bleibt. Sie bietet einige wundervolle axiale Ausblicke. Wie San Martín sagt: „Das Schönste daran ist, dass man von einer Seite zur anderen durch das ganze Haus schauen kann."

Previous pages: *The house's gallery bridges the gap between the interior and exterior. It has a fireplace and white cotton curtains, but remains open to the elements. A huge window next to the rustic dining table offers views of the sea.*
Right: *The bedside table in one of the guest suites was made by a local carpenter to the owner's design.*
Below: *A breakfast room is located next to the kitchen. The counter top is made from granite.*

Pages précédentes : *La galerie marie l'extérieur et l'intérieur. Elle possède une cheminée et des rideaux en coton blanc mais reste ouverte aux éléments. L'immense ouverture derrière la table rustique donne sur la mer.*
À droite : *La table de chevet dans l'une des suites des invités a été dessinée par la maîtresse de maison et réalisée par un artisan local.*
En bas : *La cuisine communique avec une petite pièce où l'on prend le petit-déjeuner. Le plan de travail est en granit.*

Vorhergehende Seiten: *Die Galerie des Hauses verbindet innen und außen. Sie hat einen Kamin und weiße Baumwollvorhänge, steht aber den Elementen offen. Ein riesiges Fenster beim rustikalen Esstisch gewährt Ausblick auf das Meer.*
Rechts: *Den Nachttisch in einer der Gästesuiten hat ein einheimischer Tischler nach einem Entwurf der Eigentümerin geschaffen.*
Unten: *Ein Frühstückszimmer neben der Küche. Die Arbeitsplatte dort besteht aus Granit.*

Above: Classical lines and symmetry can also be found in the living room, where two white cotton sofas flank a pair of teak sun bed bases, which act as coffee tables. The ottoman is upholstered in a hand-woven fabric made by Indians in northern Argentina. The concrete floors are decorated with geometric motifs in brick.
Right: A huge arched window affords an unobstructed view of the Atlantic from the master bed.

En haut : On retrouve les lignes classiques et la symétrie dans le séjour où deux canapés houssés de coton blanc flanquent une paire de lits de plage convertis en tables basses. Le pouf est tapissé d'une étoffe tissée par des Indiens du nord de l'Argentine. Les sols en béton sont décorés de motifs géométriques en briques.
À droite : Dans la chambre principale, une immense fenêtre cintrée donne directement sur l'Atlantique.

Oben: Klassische Linienführung und Symmetrie sind auch im Wohnzimmer zu finden: Dort flankieren zwei weiße Leinensofas die beiden Teakholzgestelle ehemaliger Sonnenliegen, die als Sofatische fungieren. Die Ottomane ist mit einem von nordargentinischen Indianern handgewebten Stoff bezogen. In die Betonböden wurden geometrische Motive aus Ziegelsteinen eingelegt.
Rechts: Ein riesiges Rundbogenfenster gewährt einen unmittelbaren Blick vom Bett des Hauptschlafzimmers auf den Atlantik.

The Customs House

La Barra, Uruguay

Pour l'architecte Martin Gomez, cette maison dans le village huppé de La Barra est doublement unique: par son emplacement sur la plage et par son histoire. Il y a un siècle, c'était un poste de douane. « Il reste peu de bâtiments aussi vieux », explique-t-il. La structure de 600 mètres carrés était « un cube aveugle ». Les ouvertures vers la mer étaient bouchées et l'intérieur rempli d'une multitude de murs. Gomez a créé de grands espaces ouverts et opté pour un décor confortable et reposant. « Je ne voulais rien d'ostentatoire. » La plupart des huit chambres ont une entrée indépendante. « C'est comme un petit hôtel. » Au milieu du jardin se dresse une terrasse en bois, « comme un radeau qu'on aurait tiré sur le rivage et abandonné sur la pelouse ».

For architect Martin Gomez, this house in the chic village of La Barra is "unique". Firstly, there is its location – right on the beach. Secondly, its history. It started out life a century ago as a customs house. "We don't have many buildings as old as this still standing," he remarks. When he first saw it, the 600-square-meter structure was "a kind of windowless cube". The openings onto the sea had been blocked up and the inside was filled with a multitude of walls. Gomez created large, open spaces, and opted for a comfortable, relaxed look. "I didn't want something ostentatious," he says. In all, there are eight bedrooms, most of which have their own separate entrance. "It's like a small hotel," he states. The deck in the middle of the garden, meanwhile, is rather like a raft. "It looks like it was dragged ashore and left in the middle of the lawn."

Für den Architekten Martin Gomez ist dieses Haus im schicken Badeort La Barra „einzigartig". Erstens wegen seiner Lage – direkt am Strand – und zweitens wegen seiner Geschichte. Ursprünglich hatte es nämlich als Zollhaus gedient. „Wir haben nicht viele Gebäude, die so alt sind wie dieses und immer noch stehen", meint er. Als er das Haus mit seiner Grundfläche von 600 Quadratmetern zum ersten Mal sah, erschien es wie „eine Art fensterloser Würfel". Die Öffnungen zum Meer waren blockiert, und im Inneren fanden sich zahlreiche Wände. Gomez schuf große offene Räume und entschied sich für einen komfortablen, entspannten Stil. „Ich wollte nichts Pompöses", sagt er. Insgesamt gibt es acht Schlafzimmer, von denen die meisten ihren eigenen Eingang besitzen. „Es ist wie ein kleines Hotel", stellt er fest. Die hölzerne Plattform mitten im Garten wirkt dagegen wie ein Floß. „Als wäre es an Land gezogen und auf dem Rasen vergessen worden."

Previous pages and above: Shade on an outdoor terrace is provided
by a roof of eucalyptus branches; the U-shaped house is centred
around a deck made from lapacho wood; inside, the atmosphere is
serene and relaxed. Furnishings include a trestle table, an old leather
chair and a sofa upholstered with hessian.
Facing page: Gomez designed the daybed and inserted blue panes
of glass into the living-room windows.
Below: Seascapes bought locally hang above a farm table in the
dining room.

Pages précédentes et en haut : Un toit en branches d'eucalyptus
ombrage la terrasse extérieure ; la maison en U est construite autour
d'une terrasse en lapacho ; à l'intérieur, l'atmosphère est sereine et
détendue. Le mobilier inclut une table posée sur des tréteaux, un
vieux fauteuil en cuir et un canapé en toile de jute.
Page de droite : Gomez a dessiné le lit de repos et inséré des pans de
verre bleus au-dessus des fenêtres du séjour.
En bas : Dans la salle à manger, des marines achetées dans la région
sont accrochées au-dessus d'une table de ferme.

Vorhergehende Seiten und oben: Die Außenterrasse erhält durch ein
Dach aus Eukalyptuszweigen Schatten; das u-förmige Haus ist um
eine zentrale Plattform aus Lapachoholz angeordnet; im Inneren
herrscht eine heiter-gelassene Atmosphäre. Zur Möblierung gehören
ein auf Böcken gestellter Tisch, ein alter Ledersessel und ein mit Sack-
leinen bezogenes Sofa.
Gegenüberliegende Seite: Gomez entwarf die Chaiselongue und versah
die Fenster des Wohnzimmers mit einem Band aus blauem Glas.
Unten: Vor Ort gekaufte Seestücke hängen über einem rustikalen
Tisch im Esszimmer.

Below: Linen curtains and Portuguese cotton bed covers in one of the guestrooms.
Following pages: The master bathroom has stucco walls and a Turkish carpet; Gomez created both the wall lights and bench on the first-floor bedroom terrace.

En bas : Dans l'une des chambres d'amis, des rideaux en lin et des dessus-de-lit portugais en coton.
Pages suivantes : Dans la chambre principale, des murs en stuc et un tapis turc ; sur la terrasse de deux chambres du premier étage, Gomez a dessiné les appliques et le banc.

Unten: Leinenvorhänge und Bettüberwurf aus portugiesischer Baumwolle in einem der Gästezimmer.
Folgende Seiten: Das Hauptbadezimmer besitzt Stuco-Wände und einen türkischen Kelim. Gomez kreierte sowohl die Wandlampen als auch die Sitzbank auf der Terrasse vor dem Schlafzimmer in der ersten Etage.

Facing page and above: The kitchen is a symphony in white. The worktops are made from Uruguayan marble and the traditional stools were created in the town of Minas.

Page de gauche et en haut : Dans la cuisine, une symphonie de blancs. Les plans de travail sont en marbre uruguayen et les tabourets traditionnels ont été fabriqués dans la ville de Minas.

Gegenüberliegende Seite und oben: Die Küche ist eine Symphonie in Weiß. Die Arbeitsflächen bestehen aus uruguayanischem Marmor, und die traditionellen Hocker wurden in der Stadt Minas angefertigt.

Hugo Ramasco

La Pedrera, Uruguay

Situé à 200 km à l'est de Montevideo, le village de La Pedrera est si petit qu'il n'y a ni banque ni bureau de poste. En revanche, sa plage de 30 km de long est bordée d'environ 180 maisons. L'une d'elles appartient au promoteur immobilier Hugo Ramasco, basé à Buenos Aires. Elle est perchée sur des pilotis en eucalyptus traité. « On l'a voulue aussi transparente que possible », explique-t-il. L'hiver, quand la mer se retire, elle se dresse sur le sable. Ceinte d'une véranda de 100 mètres carrés, elle est délibérément simple, comptant deux chambres, une salle de bains et un séjour ouvert. La plupart des meubles, dessinés par Ramasco, ont été réalisés par un menuisier du coin. La pièce principale n'a pas l'électricité. « Ainsi, le soir, on contemple la plage et la mer à la lueur des bougies. »

La Pedrera is a village some 200 kilometres east of Montevideo; it is so small that it doesn't have either a bank or a post office. It does, however, border a 30-kilometre-long beach, on which there are only about 180 houses. One of them belongs to Buenos Aires-based real-estate developer Hugo Ramasco. The structure stands on stilts made from treated eucalyptus. "We tried to make it as see-through as we could," he explains. In the winter, sand fills the area underneath. Surrounded by a 100-square-metre veranda on all four sides, the house is deliberately simple. There are two bedrooms, a bathroom and a large, open living room. Much of the furniture was designed by Ramasco and built by a local carpenter. In the main room, there isn't even electric lighting. "That way," notes Ramasco, "you look out at the beach and sea with just the glow of candles."

La Pedrera, ein Dorf etwa 200 Kilometer östlich von Montevideo, ist so klein, dass es weder eine Bank- noch eine Postfiliale besitzt. Doch es grenzt an einen 30 Kilometer langen Strand, auf dem nur 180 Häuser stehen. Eines davon gehört Hugo Ramasco, Chef einer Immobilien-firma mit Sitz in Buenos Aires. Das Bauwerk steht auf Stelzen aus behandeltem Eukalyptusholz. „Wir versuchten, es so durchlässig wie möglich zu gestalten", erklärt er. Im Winter sammelt sich Sand unter dem Boden. Auf allen vier Seiten von einer Veranda mit einer 100 Qua-dratmeter messenden Grundfläche umgeben, ist das Haus bewusst schlicht gehalten. Es gibt zwei Schlafzimmer, ein Badezimmer und einen großen offenen Wohnraum. Ein Großteil der Möbel wurde von Ramasco entworfen und von einem einheimischen Tischler gefertigt. Im Hauptwohnraum gibt es nicht einmal elektrisches Licht. „Auf diese Weise", versichert Ramasco, „lediglich im Schein von Kerzen, ist der Blick auf den Strand und das Meer umso schöner."

Previous pages: The table on the veranda was built by a local carpenter from Brazilian pine.
Above: In the open kitchen, the counter top is made from smoothed concrete and the shelf suspended from nautical ropes.
Right: The chair on the deck was bought at a craft fair in Punta del Este.

Pages précédentes : La table de la véranda a été réalisée par un artisan local en pin brésilien.
En haut : Le plateau du comptoir de la cuisine est en béton lissé. L'étagère est suspendue avec des cordes de bateau.
À droite : Le fauteuil sur la terrasse a été trouvé dans une foire artisanale à Punta del Este.

Vorhergehende Seiten: Der Tisch auf der Veranda wurde von einem einheimischen Tischler aus Tannenholz hergestellt.
Oben: In der offenen Küche besteht die Arbeitsfläche aus poliertem Beton, das Regal ist an Schiffstauen aufgehängt.
Rechts: Der Stuhl auf der Plattform stammt von einem Handwerksmarkt in Punta del Este.

Right: *Above the fireplace hangs a cement fish. The two candleholders are made from iron.*
Below: *In the seating area is a sofa made from eucalyptus and covered with canvas cushions. The pine coffee table was designed by Ramasco. The two stools come from the Compañía de Oriente in Punta del Este.*
Following pages: *Painted pine was used throughout for the interior walls. The fish skeleton is made from cement and the bedroom blind from bamboo.*

À droite : *Un poisson en ciment suspendu au-dessus de la cheminée. Les deux bougeoirs sont en fer.*
En bas : *Dans le coin salon, un canapé en eucalyptus recouvert de coussins en toile. La table basse en pin a été dessinée par Ramasco. Les deux tabourets proviennent de la Compañía de Oriente à Punta del Este.*
Pages suivantes : *À l'intérieur, les murs sont en pin peint. Dans la chambre, le squelette de poisson est en ciment et le store en bambou.*

Rechts: *Über dem Kamin hängt ein Fisch aus Zement. Die beiden Kerzenhalter sind aus Eisen.*
Unten: *Mit Segeltuch überzogene Kissen schmücken das Sofa aus Eukalyptusholz in der Sitzecke. Der Beistelltisch aus Pinienholz wurde von Ramasco entworfen. Die beiden Hocker stammen von der Compañía de Oriente in Punta del Este.*
Folgende Seiten: *Für die Innenwände wurde durchwegs gestrichenes Pinienholz verwendet. Das Fischskelett wurde aus Zement geformt, und das Rollo im Schlafzimmer besteht aus Bambus.*

Edward Rojas
Chiloé Island, Chile

L'architecte Edward Rojas était venu visiter ce palafito, une maison sur pilotis typique de l'île Chiloé, pour récupérer ses vieilles portes et fenêtres. Frappé par sa beauté, il l'a achetée tout entière. Elle se trouvait autrefois dans la montagne et a été reconstruite sur la plage où, à marée haute, elle est entourée d'eau. Bâtie au début du XXe siècle, elle possédait quatre tours qui ont été détruites par une tempête. Ses deux volumes sont reliés par une galerie en verre. « L'intérieur était rempli d'images, d'objets et de souvenirs », raconte Rojas. Il a créé la cheminée et une salle de bains, conservant les couleurs d'origine et une grande partie du mobilier. Puis il y a installé ses collections de bouteilles, de coquillages et de panneaux en métal émaillé comme celui indiquant « Señoras », qui provient d'un hôtel-restaurant de Santiago.

When architect Edward Rojas first visited this *palafito* on Chiloé Island, it was to acquire its antique doors and windows. Struck by its beauty, he decided to buy the whole house instead. *Palafito* is a term used to describe Chiloé's distinctive wooden buildings on stilts. This one was originally in the mountains. Today, it sits on the beach and at high tide is surrounded by water. Built in the early 20th century, it used to have four towers, lost in a storm. It still consists of two volumes, linked by a glass hallway. "Indoors," says Rojas, "it was full of images, objects and memories." Rojas built the firewood kitchen and a bathroom, and kept the original colours and much of the furniture. He also added collections of bottles, seashells and glazed metal signs. The one that reads "Señoras" comes from a hotel restaurant in Santiago de Chile.

Zunächst wollte der Architekt Edward Rojas nur die antiken Türen und Fenster dieses Palafito auf Chiloé Island kaufen, war jedoch so beeindruckt von der Schönheit des Hauses, dass er es ganz erwarb. Palafito ist die Bezeichnung für die landestypischen chilenischen Holzhäuser auf Stelzen. Das hier gezeigte lag ursprünglich in den Bergen. Heute steht es am Strand und ist bei Flut von Wasser umspült. Anfang des 20. Jahrhunderts erbaut, besaß es ursprünglich vier Türme, die ein Sturm davontrug. Die bestehenden zwei Baukörper sind durch einen verglasten Korridor verbunden. „Im Inneren", sagt Rojas, „war es voll von Bildern, Gegenständen und Erinnerungen." Rojas baute eine Küche mit Holzfeuerung und ein Bad ein und behielt die Farben und einen Großteil der Möbel bei. Dazu fügte er seine Sammlung von Flaschen, Muscheln und Türschildern aus lackiertem Metall. Das Schild mit der Aufschrift „Señoras" stammt aus einem Hotel-Restaurant in Santiago de Chile.

Jenny Bannister & Mongoose Belin

Lome, Australia

Elle s'appelle la Maison du pirate pour les enfants et l'Escargot en raison de sa forme en spirale pour ses propriétaires, la styliste Jenny Bannister et l'économiste Mongoose Belin. Sa façade noire s'inspire des tours en basalte de l'île Maurice et de la Réunion. Perchée sur une falaise, à deux heures au sud-ouest de Melbourne, elle est bâtie en briques en terre renforcées avec de l'asphalte. Le décor « an 1000 » a été réalisé avec des matériaux de récupération, des peaux de bêtes jetées sur les lits et les canapés, des jupettes en paille, des poignées de porte en racines de moonah. Les poutres du plafond viennent d'un embarcadère du XIXᵉ siècle et les piliers de l'escalier central d'un entrepôt de laine. Bannister collectionne les souvenirs de pirates et, quand le couple est chez lui, il hisse le pavillon noir sur le balcon.

Small children call it the "Pirate House". Owners fashion designer Jenny Bannister and economist Mongoose Belin refer to it as "Escargot" (Snail) because of its spiral form. Its black exterior was inspired by basalt towers on Mauritius and Réunion. Situated on a cliff top two hours southwest of Melbourne, the house was built from mud bricks, reinforced with asphalt. The theme for the décor was "A.D. 1000". Animal skins have been draped over beds and sofas. Salvaged materials were used throughout. Ceiling beams came from a 19th-century Melbourne pier and reclaimed timber for the central staircase from a wool storehouse. Moonah tree roots were used for door handles and grass skirts hung up throughout. Bannister also collects pirate memorabilia. Indeed, whenever the pair is in residence, they fly the Jolly Roger from a flagpole on the balcony.

Die Kinder nennen es „das Piratenhaus". Die Eigentümer, die Mode-designerin Jenny Bannister und der Ökonom Mongoose Belin, bezeichnen es wegen seiner spiralförmigen Anlage als „Escargot" („Schnecke"). Sein schwarzes Äußeres wurde von den Basalttürmen auf den Inseln Mauritius und La Réunion inspiriert. Auf einer Felskuppe zwei Stunden südwestlich von Melbourne gelegen, wurde das Haus aus mit Asphalt verputzten Lehmziegeln errichtet. Das Thema der Inneneinrichtung lautete „1000 nach Christus". Tierfelle sind über Betten und Sofas drapiert. Recyceltes fand überall Verwendung. Die Deckenbalken entstammen einem Melbourner Pier aus dem 19. Jahrhundert und die Holzbalken für die Treppe aus einem Lagerhaus für Wolle. Die Wurzeln von Moonahbäumen wurden als Türklinken verwendet, und überall wurden getrocknete Bastbüschel aufgehängt. Jenny Bannister sammelt auch Piraten-Andenken. Tatsächlich hisst das Paar, sobald es hier Quartier bezogen hat, die Totenkopfflagge der Piraten auf dem Balkon.

Left: A grass skirt has been attached to an old table in the kitchen. The cupboards are faced with wood from a paling fence and topped with shards of marble, which resemble sharks' teeth.
Below: Belin rolled vine cane into a ball to create the dramatic pendant light above the dining table.

À gauche : Dans la cuisine, une jupette en paille est accrochée au bord d'une vieille table. Les placards recouverts de bois de palissade sont couronnés d'éclats de marbre rappelant des dents de requin.
En bas : Belin a créé le lustre rond au-dessus de la table en pliant des cannes de plantes grimpantes.

Links: In der Küche schmücken getrocknete Bastbüschel einen alten Tisch. Die Küchenschränke sind mit dem Holz eines alten Lattenzauns verkleidet. An ihrer Oberkante wurden Marmor-Bruchstücke angebracht, die an Haifischzähne erinnern.
Unten: Belin rollte Weinranken zu einem Ball zusammen und schuf so den dramatischen Akzent der Hängelampe über dem Esstisch.

Previous pages: Made from mud bricks coated in black render, the house stands on a windswept coast with access to three private beaches.
Facing page: A view of the dining and kitchen area. Bannister loves the 1970s Casala chairs "because they look like whale bones". The Oregon pine and cypress dining table was made by Belin.

Pages précédentes : Réalisée en briques de terre recouvertes d'un enduit noir, la maison se dresse sur une côte balayée par le vent et jouit d'un accès à trois plages privées.
Page de gauche : La cuisine-salle à manger. Bannister adore ses chaises Casala des années 70, car « elles ressemblent à des os de baleine ». La table en pin et cyprès de l'Oregon a été réalisée par Belin.

Vorhergehende Seiten: Das aus Lehmziegeln gebaute, schwarz verputzte Haus erhebt sich auf der stürmischen Küste mit Zugang zu drei privaten Badestränden.
Gegenüberliegende Seite: Ein Blick auf den Küchen- und Essbereich. Jenny Bannister liebt die Casala-Stühle aus den 1970er-Jahren, „weil sie wie Walknochen aussehen". Der Esstisch aus Douglastanne und Zypresse wurde von Belin erbaut.

Right: Owners Mongoose Belin and Jenny Bannister taking things easy.
Below: Upstairs is one large, open-plan area. The ceiling beams come from an old Melbourne pier dating from the early 1800s. Moonah tree branches ring the stairwell.

À droite : Les propriétaires Mongoose Belin et Jenny Bannister se la coulent douce.
En bas : Une grande pièce ouverte occupe l'étage. Les poutres du plafond proviennent d'un vieil embarcadère de Melbourne, datant du début du XIXᵉ siècle. Des branches de moonah bordent la cage d'escalier.

Rechts: Die Hauseigentümer Mongoose Belin und Jenny Bannister entspannen sich.
Unten: In der oberen Etage gibt es einen großen offenen Bereich. Die Deckenbalken entstammen von einem alten Melbourner Pier aus dem frühen 19. Jahrhundert. Äste von Moonahbäumen rahmen den Treppenschacht.

Above: Animal skins abound. The rug is actually a white cow skin printed with zebra stripes. On the daybed are sheepskins, as well as cushions made from kangaroo fur printed with an ocelot motif. The 1968 "Contour Chair" is by David Colwell.
Right: The Airedale Teddy lying on a driftwood bed, that Belin made as a birthday present for Bannister.

En haut : Les peaux de bête abondent. Le tapis est en fait une peau de vache blanche imprimée de rayures de zèbre. Le lit de repos est recouvert de peau de mouton et de coussins en fourrure de kangourou imprimée d'un motif d'ocelot. La « Contour Chair » datant de 1968 est de David Colwell.
À droite : L'airedale Teddy, prend ses aises sur un lit en bois flotté réalisé par Belin en guise de cadeau d'anniversaire pour Bannister.

Oben: Tierfelle sind in Fülle vorhanden. Der Teppich ist in Wirklichkeit ein weißes, mit Zebrastreifen bedrucktes Kuhfell. Auf der Chaiselongue liegen Schaffelle und Kissen aus Kängurufell, die mit einem Ozelot-Muster bedruckt sind. Der „Contour Chair" von 1968 ist von David Colwell.
Rechts: Der Airedale-Terrier auf einem Bett aus Treibholz, das Belin als Geburtstagsgeschenk für Jenny Bannister schuf.

âFacing page: A 1960s Murano glass chandelier hangs in the bedroom. The vintage chest was originally used for storing firewood and the curtains are made from Filippino grass.

Page de droite : Dans la chambre, un lustre en verre de Murano des années 60. Le vieux coffre servait autrefois à garder des bûches. Les rideaux ont été réalisés avec des herbes sèches des Philippines.

Gegenüberliegende Seite: Eine Hängelampe aus Murano-Glas aus den 1960ern hängt im Schlafzimmer. Die alte Kommode diente ursprünglich der Aufbewahrung von Feuerholz; die Vorhänge bestehen aus Filipinogras.

Above: The spiral staircase was inspired by those in medieval French châteaux. The stairs were made from reclaimed wood from a wool storehouse and the railing from hollow bent steel.
Right: A console table was made from the off-cuts of three slabs of wood used for the stairs.

En haut : L'escalier en colimaçon s'inspire de ceux des châteaux médiévaux français. Les marches ont été taillées dans du bois récupéré dans un ancien entrepôt de laine. La rampe est en tubes d'acier creux.
À droite : Une console réalisée avec les restes de trois blocs de bois utilisés pour les marches.

Oben: Die Wendeltreppe ist inspiriert von Treppen mittelalterlicher französischer Châteaux. Die Stufen wurden aus dem restaurierten Holz eines alten Lagerhauses für Wolle gefertigt, das Geländer ist aus Schmiedeeisen.
Rechts: Ein Konsolentischchen entstand aus den Abfällen von drei für die Treppe genutzten Holzbalken.

New Seaside Interiors   Jenny Bannister & Mongoose Belin

St Andrews
Residence

Mornington Peninsula, Australia

L'architecte Nik Karalis qualifie sa demeure de vacances de « réinter-
prétation de la maison australienne dans un environnement inhospi-
talier » ; en l'occurrence, les dunes sauvages de la péninsule de
Mornington, à 70 km de Melbourne. « Dans ce paysage ouvert à
l'infini, pas question de tout aplanir », explique-t-il. Il a donc posé
sa structure de trois pièces sur une plateforme flottante en béton,
soutenue par des piliers de 6 m de haut afin que les dunes puissent
se mouvoir librement autour et dessous. Les deux façades sont diffé-
rentes. Celle donnant sur le nord, à laquelle on accède par une rampe,
est tapissée de bardeaux en jarrah, un bois local. Celle donnant sur le
sud est percée d'une immense baie vitrée qui vous met en contact
direct avec la nature. « Le maison vous oblige à vous concentrer sur
la vue ; vous ne pouvez pas y échapper. »

Architect Nik Karalis calls his holiday home "a new interpretation
of the Australian house in the challenging landscape". The landscape in question is the Mornington Peninsula some 70 kilometres
from Melbourne with its rugged sand dunes. "The terrain is unin-
terrupted," he asserts. "So, the last thing you want to do is to go in
and level everything." Instead, he placed the two-bedroom house
on six-metre screw piles, which support a floating concrete platform.
That way, the dunes can move freely around and underneath it. The
two façades are deliberately different. The north one, accessed by
a ramp, is clad in local jarrah wood. The south one is punctured
with an enormous, full-length glazed window, which places you in
direct contact with nature. As Karalis says: "The house forces you
to focus on the landscape. You simply can't escape it."

Der Architekt Nik Karalis nennt sein Ferienhaus „eine Neuinterpreta-
tion des australischen Hauses angesichts der Herausforderungen der
Landschaft". Letztere ist die etwa 70 Kilometer von Melbourne ent-
fernte Halbinsel Mornington mit ihren buckligen Sanddünen. „Das
Terrain befindet sich ständig in Bewegung", versichert Nik. „Daher ist
das Letzte, was man tun möchte, alles einzuebnen." Stattdessen
stellte er das Haus auf sechs Meter hohe, in den Boden gerammte
Metallpfeiler, die eine schwebende Betonplattform tragen. So haben
die Dünen freien Spielraum neben und unter dem Haus. Die beiden
Fassaden wurden bewusst unterschiedlich gestaltet. Die über eine
Rampe erreichbare Nordseite ist mit einheimischem Jarrahholz verkleidet. Die Südfront bildet ein riesiges raumhohes Glasfenster, das
den Bewohner in unmittelbaren Kontakt zur Natur bringt. Karalis
sagt: „Das Haus zwingt einen, sich auf die Landschaft zu konzen-
trieren. Man kann ihr nicht entkommen."

Previous pages: *The iconic "La Chaise" by Charles and Ray Eames stands in front of the spectacular view over the dunes of the Mornington Peninsula.*
Above: *The south façade is a 30-metre-long wall of glass.*
Right: *The steps leading down to the dunes were made from an indigenous hardwood called jarrah.*

Pages précédentes : *La célèbre « Chaise » de Charles et Ray Eames devant la vue spectaculaire sur les dunes de la péninsule de Mornington.*
En haut : *La façade donnant sur le sud est composée d'un mur de verre de 30 m de long.*
À droite : *Les marches menant aux dunes ont été réalisées en jarrah, un bois indigène.*

Vorhergehende Seiten: *Die Stuhlikone „La Chaise" von Charles und Ray Eames vor der spektakulären Aussicht über die Dünen der Halbinsel Mornington.*
Oben: *Eine 30 Meter lange Wand aus Glas bildet die Südfassade.*
Rechts: *Die zu den Dünen hinabführenden Stufen wurden aus dem harten Holz des einheimischen Jarrahbaums gefertigt.*

Right: Karalis designed the kitchen himself. The Carrara marble counter is set on a stainless-steel base. The tap is manufactured by Vola.
Below: Eames fibreglass dining chairs, Alvar Aalto stools and an Edra ottoman in the open-plan living room.
Following pages: The custom-made cabinet in the master bedroom was made from painted MDF; visitors discover the view of the sea when they arrive at the main entrance.

À droite : Karalis a dessiné lui-même la cuisine. Le comptoir en marbre de Carrare est posé sur un support en acier inoxydable. La robinetterie vient de chez Vola.
En bas : Dans le séjour ouvert, des chaises en fibres de verre des Eames, des tabourets d'Alvar Aalto et un pouf de chez Edra.
Pages suivantes : Le meuble blanc au pied du lit est en médium peint. Les visiteurs découvrent la mer dès qu'ils franchissent l'entrée principale.

Rechts: Karalis hat die Küche selbst entworfen. Die Platte aus Carrara-Marmor ruht auf einem Sockel aus Edelstahl. Der Wasserhahn ist von Vola.
Unten: Esstischstühle aus Fiberglas von Eames. Alvar-Aalto-Hocker und eine Edra-Ottomane im offen gestalteten Wohnzimmer.
Folgende Seiten: Der maßgefertigte Kasten am Bettende im Schlafzimmer wurde aus gestrichenen MDF-Platten gefertigt; sobald man den Haupteingang erreicht, öffnet sich der Ausblick aufs Meer.

Ken Crosson

Coromandel Peninsula,
New Zealand

« Ayant grandi dans une ferme, j'ai voulu me rapprocher de la nature et offrir à mes enfants la même vie saine », explique l'architecte Ken Crosson. Il a conçu sa maison de vacances, bâtie sur un site isolé (à 20 km de la ville la plus proche), sobre et « régionale », renonçant à la plupart des commodités modernes : pas de lave-vaisselle, de télé ni d'ordinateur. S'inspirant des barrages à bascule construits par les bûcherons au XIXᵉ siècle, il a tapissé la structure de bardeaux en cyprès de Lawson et l'a équipée de terrasses qui se relèvent pour fermer la maison quand la famille n'est pas là. Toutefois, le plus original, c'est la baignoire sur roulettes que l'on remplit à l'intérieur puis que l'on pousse où l'on veut. « On peut prendre son bain devant la cheminée ou sous les étoiles. » Ça, c'est ce qui s'appelle un vrai retour à la nature.

"I grew up on a farm and wanted to get back to nature and give my kids something like the lifestyle I'd enjoyed in childhood," declares architect Ken Crosson. The site he chose for the family's holiday home is certainly remote (the nearest town is 20 kilometres away). He also eschewed many mod cons. There is no dishwasher, TV or computer. Crosson's intent was to create something "gutsy" and "regional". He took inspiration from local wooden "trip" dams built by 19th-century loggers and clad the house in Lawson's cypress. He also fitted it with two decks, which can be raised to shut up the house when the family is not there. The most unusual element, however, is the bathtub on wheels, which can be filled inside and then pushed around. "You can have a bath in front of the fire or under the stars," enthuses Crosson. How's that for getting back to nature?

„Ich bin auf einer Farm aufgewachsen und wollte zurück zur Natur und meinen Kindern einen ähnlichen Lebensstil bieten, wie ich ihn als Kind erleben durfte", erklärt der Architekt Ken Crosson. Das Grundstück, das er für das Ferienhaus der Familie auswählte, ist auf jeden Fall sehr abgelegen, die nächste Stadt liegt 20 Kilometer entfernt. Außerdem verzichtete er auf viel modernen Komfort. Es gibt keine Geschirrspülmaschine, keinen Fernseher oder Computer. Crosson wollte etwas „Uriges" und „Landestypisches" schaffen. Er ließ sich von den Dammwegen der Holzfäller des 19. Jahrhunderts inspirieren und verkleidete das Haus mit dem Holz von Lawson-Zypressen. Auch mit zwei hölzernen Plattformen stattete er es aus, die hochgezogen werden können und das Haus einschließen, wenn die Familie abwesend ist. Das ungewöhnlichste Element ist jedoch die Badewanne auf Rädern. „Man kann vor dem Kamin oder unter dem Sternenhimmel baden", schwärmt Crosson. Wenn das kein Zurück zur Natur ist!

Previous pages: Two "Butterfly" chairs look out towards the beach and sea.
Right: Crosson chose the manuka-clad site because of its remoteness. The only other houses on the beach are a few cabana-style bachs.
Below: The house is clad in Lawson's cypress. The decks can be raised with electric winches to close up the house when the family is not in residence.

Pages précédentes : Deux fauteuils « Butterfly » d'où savourer la vue sur la plage et la mer.
À droite : Crosson a choisi ce site envahi de manuka en raison de son isolement. Les seules autres maisons qui se trouvent ici sont des cabanes de plage.
En bas : La maison est tapissée de bardeaux en cyprès de Lawson. Des treuils électriques permettent de rabattre les terrasses pour fermer la maison quand la famille ne l'utilise pas.

Vorhergehende Seiten: Zwei „Butterfly"-Stühle mit dem Ausblick auf Strand und Meer.
Rechts: Crosson wählte das mit Manuka-Sträuchern bedeckte Grundstück wegen seiner Abgeschiedenheit. Die einzigen anderen Häuser am Strand sind ein paar vereinzelte Hütten.
Unten: Das Haus ist mit dem Holz von Lawson-Zypressen verkleidet. Die Plattformen kann man mithilfe von elektrischen Winden wie eine Zugbrücke hochziehen, um das Haus abzuschließen, wenn die Familie nicht da ist.

Above: Riccardo Blumer's "Laleggera" chairs flank an oak dining table designed by Crosson.
Right: The bedroom windows are fitted with solid shutters, which fold down to enclose both ends of the house.
Following pages: Hoop pine plywood was used for the kitchen cabinets. The fireplace is made from steel plate and the Crosson-designed master bed from Lawson's cypress. The steel-framed bathtub can be wheeled outside for an open-air soak. Afterwards, the water drains through the cracks of the deck.

En haut : Autour d'une table en chêne dessinée par Crosson, des chaises « Laleggera » de Riccardo Blumer.
À droite : Les fenêtres des chambres sont équipées de robustes volets qui s'abaissent pour fermer les deux extrémités de la maison.
Pages suivantes : Les placards de la cuisine sont en contreplaqué de pin de Hoop. La cheminée a été réalisée avec des plaques d'acier et le lit de la chambre principale, dessiné par Crosson, en cyprès de Lawson. La baignoire, montée sur une structure en acier, peut être poussée à l'extérieur pour une trempette en plein air. L'eau s'écoule ensuite entre les lattes de la terrasse en bois.

Oben: Riccardo Blumers „Laleggera"-Stühle flankieren einen von Crosson entworfenen Esstisch aus Eichenholz.
Rechts: Die Schlafzimmerfenster sind mit soliden Fensterläden ausgestattet, die beim Zuklappen die Hausfassade nahtlos abschließen.
Folgende Seiten: Schuppentannen-Sperrholz wurde für die Küchenschränke verwendet. Der Kamin besteht aus Stahl und das von Crosson entworfene Doppelbett aus dem Holz von Lawson-Zypressen. Die stahlgerahmte Badewanne lässt sich nach draußen rollen. Nach dem Bad im Freien fließt das Wasser durch die Spalten der Plattform ab.

Addresses / Adresses / Adressen

TODD SAUNDERS &
TOMMIE WILHELMSEN,
HARDANGER, NORWAY
Saunders Architecture
Vestre torggate 22
5015 Bergen
Norway
phone: +47 55 36 85 06
post@saunders.no
www.saunders.no

HANNE KJÆRHOLM,
RUNGSTED KYST, DENMARK
Hanne Kjærholm
Overgaden Oven Vandet 8
1415 Copenhagen K.
Denmark
phone: +45 32 57 34 82
www.dronningerne.dk

BLACK RUBBER BEACH
HOUSE, DUNGENESS
BEACH, ENGLAND
Simon Conder Associates Ltd.
Nile Street Studios
8 Nile Street
London N1 7RF
United Kingdom
phone: +44 20 72 51 21 44
sca@simonconder.co.uk
www.simonconder.co.uk

SEASIDE SIMPLICITY,
KNOKKE-ZOUTE, BELGIUM
Vincent Van Duysen Architects
Lombardenvest 34
2000 Antwerp
Belgium
phone: +32 3 20 59 190
vincent@vincentvanduysen.
com
www.vincentvanduysen.com

PIERRE CARDIN,
SAINT-TROPEZ, FRANCE
Jean-Michel Ducancelle
2, route de Toucheronde
49800 Andard
France
phone: +33 2 44 61 21 41
jean-michel@ducancelle.com

KRIS RUHS,
PORTOFINO, ITALY
Kris Ruhs
Corso Como 10
20154 Milan
Italy
phone: +39 02 54 64 589
kr@galleriacarlasozzani.org
www.krisruhs.com

DOLCE & GABBANA,
PORTOFINO, ITALY
Dolce & Gabbana
Via Goldoni 10
20129 Milano
Italy
phone: +39 02 77 42 71
www.dolcegabbana.it

Ferruccio Laviani
Via De Amicis 53
20123 Milano
Italy
phone: +39 02 89 42 14 26
info@laviani.com
www.laviani.com

FIONA SWAROVSKI,
CAPRI, ITALY
Fiona Winter Studio
Via Felice Casati 2
20124 Milan
Italy
phone: +39 02 20 56 94 206
office@fionawinterstudio.com
www.fionawinterstudio.com

TILED TREASURE,
POSITANO, ITALY
Lazzarini Pickering Architetti
Via Cola di Rienzo 28
00192 Rome
Italy
phone: +39 06 32 10 305
info@lazzarinipickering.com
www.lazzarinipickering.com

BELQUIS ZAHIR,
FILICUDI, ITALY
Belquis Zahir
belquis_z@hotmail.com

PAUL BARTHELEMY,
ALICUDI, ITALY
Paul Barthelemy
Via Roma 3
95027 San Gregorio di Catania
Italy
phone: +39 09 57 21 16 14
paul.barthelemy@tin.it

JOSÉ GANDÍA-BLASCO,
IBIZA, SPAIN
Gandia Blasco S.A.
Músico Vert, 4
46870 Ontinyent
Valencia
Spain
phone: +34 902 53 03 02
info@gandiablasco.com
www.gandiablasco.com

JACQUES GRANGE,
CARVALHAL, PORTUGAL
Jacques Grange
21, rue Bouloi
75001 Paris
France
phone: +33 1 55 80 75 40
contact@jacquesgrange.com

GIANNA & THEODORE
ANGELOPOULOS,
MYKONOS, GREECE
Alberto Pinto
Hôtel de la Victoire
11, rue d'Aboukir
75002 Paris
France
phone: +33 1 40 13 00 00
contact@albertopinto.com
www.albertopinto.com

YORGOS ZAPHIRIOU,
SERIFOS, GREECE
Yorgos Zaphiriou
8, Pittakoy Street
10558 Athens
Greece
phone: +30 210 32 33 753
g-z@otenet.gr

ALAN WANZENBERG,
FIRE ISLAND, NEW YORK
Alan Wanzenberg
333 West 52nd Street
New York, NY 10019
United States
phone: +1 212 489 7980
www.alanwanzenberg.com

ANNABELLE SELLDORF,
LONG ISLAND, NEW YORK
Selldorf Architects
860 Broadway
New York, NY 10003
United States
phone: +1 212 219 9571
info@selldorf.com
www.selldorf.com

LISA PERRY,
SAG HARBOR, NEW YORK
Lisa Perry Studio
383 West Broadway
New York, NY 10012
United States
phone: +1 212 334 1956
www.lisaperrystyle.com

DANIELLE & DAVID GANEK,
SOUTHAMPTON,
NEW YORK
Fox-Nahem Design
82 East 10th Street
New York, NY 10003
United States
phone: +1 212 358 1411
info@foxnahemdesign.com
www.foxnahemdesign.com

SHORE CHIC,
MARTHA'S VINEYARD,
MASSACHUSETTS
Paula Perlini Inc.
165 East 35th Street
New York, NY 10016
United States
phone: +1 212 889 6551
pperlininc@aol.com
www.paulaperlini.com

Ferguson & Shamamian
Architects
270 Lafayette Street
Suite 300
New York, NY 10012
United States
phone: +1 212 941 8088
www.fergusonshamamian.com

BARBARA BECKER,
MIAMI, FLORIDA
Oscar Glottman
4141 NE 2 Avenue
Miami, FL 33137
United States
phone: +1 305 438 3711
info@glottman.com
www.glottman.com

MARBRISA,
ACAPULCO, MEXICO
Lautner Associates-Helena
Arahuete Architect
8055 W. Manchester Avenue
Suite 705
Playa Del Rey, CA 90293
United States
phone: +1 310 577 7783
lautnerassoc@earthlink.net
www.lautnerassociates.com

Escher GuneWardena
Architecture
815 Silver Lake Boulevard
Los Angeles, CA 90026
United States
phone: +1 323 665 9100
info@egarch.net
www.egarch.net

MIMA & CÉSAR REYES,
NAGUABO, PUERTO RICO
Jorge Pardo Sculpture
5305 Alhambra Avenue
Los Angeles, CA 90032
United States
phone: +1 323 225 4717
jps@jorgepardosculpture.com
www.jorgepardosculpture.com

RUDOLF NUREYEV,
SAINT BARTHS,
FRENCH WEST INDIES
Maison Noureev
nar@noureev.com

DAAN NELEMANS,
MANZANILLO, COSTA RICA
Daan Nelemans
phone: +506 75 99 016
info@congo-bongo.com
www.congo-bongo.com

WHITE WONDER,
IPORANGA, BRAZIL
Isay Weinfeld
Rua Andre Fernandes 175
Itaim-Bibi 04536.020
São Paulo SP
Brazil
phone: +55 11 30 79 75 81
info@isayweinfeld.com
www.isayweinfeld.com

AZUL GARCÍA URIBURU,
FARO JOSÉ IGNACIO,
URUGUAY
Azul García Uriburu
Martin Coronado 3117
Capital Federal (1425)
Buenos Aires
Argentina
phone: +54 11 48 02 93 28
azulgu@reservaelpotrero.
com.ar
www.azulgarciauriburu.com.ar

MICHEL GRETHER,
PUNTA DEL ESTE, URUGUAY
Michel Grether
Av. Libertador 2306, 1A
1425 Buenos Aires
Argentina
phone: +54 11 44 47 14 14
grethermichel@hotmail.com

COOL CLASSICISM,
MANANTIALES, URUGUAY
San Martín-Lonné Arquitectos
Parana 759 1° Piso
C.P. C1017AAN
Buenos Aires
Argentina
phone: +54 11 43 72 39 38
estudio@sanmartinlonne.
com.ar
www.sanmartinlonne.com.ar

THE CUSTOMS HOUSE,
LA BARRA, URUGUAY
Martin Gomez Arquitectos
Ruta 10, km 161
La Barra
Maldonado
Uruguay
phone: +598 42 77 20 04
estudio@martingomezarqui-
tectos.com
www.martingomezarquitectos.
com

EDWARD ROJAS,
CHILOÉ ISLAND, CHILE
Edward Rojas Arquitecto
Pasaje Díaz 181
Castro
Chile
phone: +56 65 63 39 62
edwardrojasvega@gmail.com
www.edwardrojas.cl

JENNY BANNISTER &
MONGOOSE BELIN,
LOME, AUSTRALIA
Jenny Bannister
jennyban@bigpond.net.au

ST ANDREWS RESIDENCE,
MORNINGTON PENINSULA,
AUSTRALIA
Nik Karalis
Woods Bagot
The Beacon Podium
Level 1
3 Southgate Avenue
Southbank
Melbourne, Victoria 3000
Australia
phone: +61 3 86 46 66 00
wbmel@woodsbagot.com
www.woodsbagot.com.au

KEN CROSSON,
COROMANDEL PENINSULA,
NEW ZEALAND
Crosson Clarke Carnachan
Architects
Level 1
15 Bath Street
PO Box 37-521
Parnell
Auckland
New Zealand
phone: +64 93 02 02 22
architects@ccca.co.nz
www.ccca.co.nz